DESPERATELY SEEKING SOLUTIONS
RATIONING HEALTH CARE

Desperately Seeking Solutions
Rationing Health Care

David J. Hunter

Routledge
Taylor & Francis Group

LONDON AND NEW YORK

First published 1997 by Pearson Education Limited

Published 2014 by Routledge
2 Park Square, Milton Park, Abingdon, Oxon OX14 4RN
711 Third Avenue, New York, NY 10017 USA

Routledge is an imprint of the Taylor & Francis Group, an informa business

ISBN: 978-1-315-84227-1 (eISBN)

ISBN 978-0-582-28923-9

British Library Cataloguing-in-Publication Data
A catalogue record for this book is available from the British Library

Library of Congress Cataloging-in-Publication Data
Hunter, David J.
    Desperately seeking solutions : rationing health care / David J.
Hunter.
        p.   cm.
    Includes bibliographical references and index.
    ISBN 0–582–28923–8 (pbk.)
    1. Health care rationing–Great Britain.   2. Health care
rationing.   I. Title.
RA410.55.G7H86   1997
362.1'0941–dc21   97–28451
                                                                    CIP

Set by 35 in 10/11pt Times

To Eve and Miles

Health policy is pathological because we are neurotic, and we insist on making our government psychotic. Our neurosis consists in knowing what is required for good health (Mother was right: Eat a good breakfast! Sleep eight hours a day! Don't drink! Don't smoke! Keep clean! And don't worry!) but not being willing to do it. Government's ambivalence consists of paying both coming and going: once for telling citizens how to be healthy, and once for paying people's bills when this goes unheeded. Psychosis appears when government persists in repeating this self-defeating play. Maybe 21st century people will come to cherish their absurdities.

Wildavsky (1979: 307–8)

It rarely occurs to contributors to the debate that the questions under discussion cannot be answered. The assumption that acceptable answers *can* be found is a pre-condition of participation in the debate.

Loughlin (1996: 147)

Society must not insulate itself from the agony of each decision to forgo beneficial treatment as it is experienced by patients, families, and care givers. If rationing is only the impersonal application of a rule to a faceless group, we risk an ever-expanding set of exclusions . . . from medical care as costs increase.

Levinsky (1990: 1815)

CONTENTS

PREFACE

This book has been a long time gestating. It originated in a short research paper commissioned by the National Association of Health Authorities and Trusts (NAHAT), as it then was, and published in 1993, on rationing dilemmas in health care. Philip Hunt, NAHAT's Director, was concerned that the manner in which rationing was being discussed in the UK and the solutions being propounded to address the dilemmas it posed could destroy the NHS. Loose talk about rationing could, he believed, play into the hands of those who wished to see the NHS reduced to a safety net for the poor and needy. If anything, that concern is even more acute as I write.

In the light of these concerns, my brief was to examine critically the rationing 'debate' such as it was at the time and to offer an antidote or countervailing view to the somewhat hysterical outbursts of those who not only wanted government to confront the hard choices in health care but who, presumably in order to advance their cause, dangerously over-simplified some rather complex issues while overlooking others. I suggested, a trifle provocatively perhaps, that the manner in which rationing was being pursued in Britain gave grounds for concern because important aspects 'are being overlooked wilfully or summarily dismissed' with the result 'that some over-hasty and rash initiatives may be launched which will almost certainly have undesirable consequences and lead to bad decisions' (Hunter 1993a: 5).

My review was not intended to be a defence of the prevailing system of professional paternalism. I simply sought to provide, as I do in this book in expanded form, a more realistic assessment than has hitherto been forthcoming of the complexities involved in moving from a form of implicit to explicit rationing and the implications of doing so for all those involved in providing and receiving health care. My principal aim, as it is here, was to raise critical awareness of the subject and to offer a perspective which was distinctive and did not merely follow the proselytizers of hard choices and rational rationing.

It is because I believe the rational rationers to be fundamentally misguided and politically naïve, but also to be the harbingers of the NHS's possible demise, however unintentionally, that I have written this book. At a time, with the NHS approaching its fiftieth birthday, when the views of the rational rationers appear to be in the ascendancy, there is a pressing need for a countervailing set of arguments and an alternative policy perspective. Regrettably, though not surprisingly, the media are not providing any sense of balance or desire to grapple with the complexities of the issue of rationing. The considerable interest they have shown in the subject has been typically emotional, selective and partisan and has probably done more to confuse than to inform or enlighten. The worst offenders, in my view, have been the specialist health correspondents who surely ought to know better.

Since embarking on this project two books on the same subject (New and Le Grand 1996; Klein *et al.* 1996) and countless journal articles have appeared. Inevitably there is some overlap between them and the contents of this book. However, where I believe this text to be distinctive is in its critique of the 'hard choices' brigade, or rational rationers, who appear to dominate the public debate about health-care rationing. It also seeks to map out an alternative prescription from that expounded by those who advocate explicit rationing based on a leadership role for central government.

Like rationing itself, writing a book is not a painless activity. There are costs, chief among these being a neglect of my family. So I am indebted to Jacqui, Eve and Miles to whom I dedicate this book as a small token of my appreciation. I could not have made the necessary sacrifice without their full and unstinting support and encouragement. Nor would the book have been possible without first-class and speedy word-processing support from Carol Ward and from Annie Flanagan who took over from Carol towards the end of the process. I should also like to thank Lorraine Bate and the staff of the Information Resource Centre at the Nuffield Institute for invaluable assistance with the literature search. This book has been informed in all kinds of ways by my experience as an observer of the NHS over many years both as someone on the edges of policy and practice and also as a part-time insider for the past five years or so in my capacity as a health authority non-executive director. Over the years, many individuals in and around the NHS have influenced my thinking and helped shape my views on rationing. They are too numerous to name individually and are doubtless unaware of any impact they might have had. But I thank them all for their contribution to this book. Of course, when all is said and done, the views expressed herein are entirely my own.

David J. Hunter
Professor of Health Policy and Management
Nuffield Institute for Health
University of Leeds
April 1997

ACKNOWLEDGEMENTS

We are grateful to the following for permission to reproduce copyright material: Ministry of Welfare, Health and Cultural Affairs, The Netherlands, for a figure from *Choices in Health Care. A Report by the Government Committee on Choices in Health Care, The Netherlands* (1992); Radcliffe Medical Press for a figure from *Priority Setting in Action: Purchasing Dilemmas* by F. Honigsbaum, J. Richards and T. Lockett (1995a). Grateful thanks also go to Lawrence Malcolm, Professor Emeritus, Community Health, University of Otago, New Zealand, and to Tom Van der Grinten Professor of Health Care Policy and Organization, Erasmus University, Rotterdam, The Netherlands for their helpful comments on the sections on priority-setting in New Zealand and The Netherlands respectively in Chapter 5.

PART ONE

The Dilemma of Rationing Health Care: Origins and Definitions

CHAPTER 1

Introduction

When the case of Child B hit the headlines and came to national prominence in Britain in 1995, it dramatically put the issue of health-care rationing before the public and firmly on the political agenda (see Box 1.1). Whatever the rights and wrongs of the affair and the way it proceeded (Cambridge and Huntingdon Health Commission was praised by ministers for its sensitive but firm handling of the issue) it did achieve one thing: it exploded the myth that the National Health Service (NHS) was prepared to fund any treatment, especially one that was essentially untried and experimental. The Child B case was an example of decision-making that sought to be principled and informed by expert opinion and evidence which suggested that to proceed with treatment would neither be cost-effective nor enhance the patient's quality of life. The case, and the emotions it aroused, were a perfect demonstration of the complexities and dilemmas which abound in all such individual circumstances.

There are no right answers in such cases – only individuals both inside and outside the NHS groping for a defensible solution while, at the same time, desperate to find one. But this did not prevent many onlookers from insisting that there was a right answer. The problem is there were so many so-called 'right' answers ranging from the decision the health authority made at one extreme to the view that a better funded service would not have necessitated such a denial of treatment, regardless of its experimental and unproven nature, at the other extreme.

There will be many more cases like Child B. Whether they will be handled any differently will depend on the individual circumstances surrounding each case and on how rationing is viewed at the time by politicians, local practitioners and managers, and the public. Are such decisions to be left to individual health authorities, and their medical advisers, to resolve as they judge appropriate, as the previous (and probably also the present) government considered to be the correct way to proceed (Secretary of State for Health 1996)? Are they to occur within a nationally determined explicit framework or set of rules governing decision-making in such cases? Or will it be decreed that the NHS will only cover particular core services and will exclude a range of treatments and interventions which can only be obtained through private means? Each position has its pros and cons as well as its supporters and detractors. It is the purpose of this book to tease out, and explore systematically, all these matters to aid understanding of both

Box 1.1 The case of Child B

In March 1995, Child B – a 10-year-old girl suffering from leukaemia – became the subject of a legal action brought by her father against Cambridge Health Authority's (now Cambridge and Huntingdon Health Commission) decision to refuse to spend £75 000 on further treatment for the girl. The High Court of Appeal ruled that the health authority had acted rationally and fairly in reaching its decision.

The case is notable because it had all the ingredients of a classic example of health-care rationing. It was a matter of life and death and brought to public attention the daily decisions made by doctors about who to treat and how. Views were sharply polarized: some supported the health authority's decision while others (probably the majority) argued that Child B should receive whatever treatment was available regardless of cost and the unproven nature of the treatment.

The facts of the case are these. The girl – Jaymee Bowen – had been diagnosed as suffering from leukaemia in 1990. She was given two rounds of chemotherapy and a bone-marrow transplant was carried out in 1994. She suffered a relapse in January 1995. The possibility of further treatment – chemotherapy possibly followed by a second transplant – was discussed. But the doctor, supported by other specialists, judged that there was little to gain from subjecting Child B to further suffering when the prospects for success were so slight: probably no more than 10 per cent. The father did not accept this judgement. He found a private specialist prepared to treat Child B who put the chance of success at around 20 per cent. But the health authority refused to pay for the proposed treatment which prompted the father to appeal to the courts. Although the father lost, a private benefactor provided the cost of treatment. In the event, despite further treatment, Child B died in May 1996.

the rationing issue in health care and the attempts by governments of all political persuasions in the UK and overseas to find an appropriate policy response.

As events subsequently proved, this book was written during the final months of the Conservative government's term of office although this was not known for certain until 2 May 1997 when a new Labour government assumed office after the Conservative Party suffered a resounding defeat in the general election held on 1 May. For some 18 years, UK health policy had been shaped and reshaped by Conservative ideology and values. During this period, the NHS was reorganized on successive occasions and its management arrangements and systems strengthened.

With the new Labour government just over a month old (at the time of writing), its health policy remains unclear and is still evolving. Apart from a wish to end the NHS internal market and commitments to honour the previous government's expenditure plans, reduce management costs and reduce waiting lists, the government's promises are few and imprecise. On many issues – notably the development of a primary care-led NHS – the new government's position is little different from its predecessor. On issues like rationing, the government has yet to adopt or declare its position. It will need to do so at some stage soon because pressures on resources are intensifying. Unless new money is to be found or imaginative ways of using existing resources identified, the government will find itself being heavily lobbied by professional bodies and others to define what the NHS will and will not cover. Although the Labour government could adopt the position maintained by the former Conservative government, which was to resist repeated calls to lead a national debate on rationing and not to have an explicit national policy on the subject, it might find such a stance uncomfortable and in conflict with its commitment to a National Health Service in which notions of equity and social justice are uppermost as central principles to be enshrined in health policy and defended in its implementation. However, for reasons explored in this book, and despite its quite different principles and values, it may well prove to be the case that Labour will not adopt a markedly different stance from its predecessor on the subject of health-care rationing. Of course, a dramatic new departure cannot be ruled out in the case of a government which has already demonstrated its capacity to surprise and do the unexpected. But the NHS and Labour are bound up in all kinds of ways and while that can, paradoxically, create the circumstances to be radical and bold, it also makes for caution and a reluctance to do anything that might smack of a betrayal of the NHS's founding principles to provide comprehensive care to all those in need of it. As this book argues, even if it were to be a credible, legitimate and ethical position to adopt there is little to be gained politically by a government seeking to be rational and explicit about rationing.

Rationing: the health policy challenge

Health care systems everywhere are experiencing a series of policy dilemmas. None of these is especially new, even if packaged and presented as such, but governments continue to wrestle with them in an attempt to find a 'right' answer as if it were axiomatic that one existed somewhere waiting to be discovered. It is conceivable, and probably the case, that no 'right' answer or lasting solution exists and that the challenge facing governments is not to conduct a futile, and ultimately illusory, search for one but rather to seek an acceptable accommodation between various competing pressures and to ensure that the means exist to allow such an outcome to occur. In fact, in Simon's words, policy-makers generally 'satisfice' and adopt an approach based on 'bounded rationality' despite the pretence that they act and behave optimally (Simon 1957). In plain language, they do not seek perfection, which is unattainable, but are in practice content to settle for less imperfection.

A difficulty confronting policy-makers is that they rarely wish to acknowledge publicly any limitations on their ability to act decisively or rationally even if, privately, 'satisficing' describes precisely how they behave and conduct their business. They are, therefore, forever put in the position of desperately seeking (rational) solutions to the 'possibly unwinnable dilemmas of social policy' (Heclo 1975: 152).

Rationing health care, it will be argued, is *par excellence* one of those unwinnable dilemmas, transcending the different funding and structural arrangements which countries have adopted and adapted for their respective health-care systems. Whatever the terminology employed to describe the activity – and less pejorative alternatives to rationing are 'priority-setting' and 'making choices' – its implications are clear enough. There are, it is asserted, simply not enough resources (financial and human) to meet all the demands placed upon them and there are never likely to be. If no controls or boundaries are placed on the public's seemingly voracious appetite for health care then a country's whole GNP could be consumed by health care with one half of the population looking after the other half. The dilemma is that more is unlikely to mean better and is neatly summed up in Wildavsky's phrase: 'doing better and feeling worse' (Wildavsky 1979). No matter what resources are allocated to health care, and regardless of the increased activity obtained from these, they are never likely to be sufficient to keep pace with growing needs and demands. Resources are finite, it is alleged, whereas needs, and certainly demands and wants, are infinite.

Need versus demand

There are fierce divisions of opinion on this issue which will be explored later in the book. But the line-up of contestants looks something like this: first, there are those who distinguish between need and demand, arguing that need is finite while conceding that demand is probably infinite and that the job of a public health-care system is to concentrate on need, not demand; and then there are those who believe that the present level of funding on health care may be sufficient to meet legitimate claims on them or even too generous, rather than deficient, as various vested interests and the media would have us believe, and that before considering demands for new resources for health-care services there is a prior need to be sure that such investment will demonstrably improve health status. For this second group, which also happens to come closest to the British government's position, explicit, hard-nosed rationing is seen to be a desperate act: an admission of failure to manage resources wisely by, *inter alia*, failing to concentrate existing and new investment on effective medical interventions and to disinvest in those shown to be ineffective. Evidence-based medicine (EBM) represents the 'new rationality' for this group. To talk of rationing in advance of rooting out as far as possible all known ineffective practices is defeatist, premature and unethical. Critics of this somewhat Utopian view of the place of, and prospects for, EBM call for a more cautious approach and an acknowledgement of the complexities and limitations of EBM (Hunter 1995b; Tanenbaum 1995; Klein 1996; Charlton 1997). Quite apart from the difficulties confronting researchers in terms of acquiring sound data and information, there are major barriers to be overcome about how the evidence is then applied in practice. In the NHS's Research and Development strategy, from which EBM has sprung, the 'D' is as important as the 'R'. These issues are taken up in Chapter 4.

Whatever the outcome of the debate over whether or not need and/or demand are finite or infinite, the present orthodoxy or conventional wisdom in all political systems is that difficult choices have to be taken about who to include and treat, and who to exclude and not treat. Few, other than those who challenge the very premises on which the debate is founded, deny that this is the case. Debate, often heated, is confined to *who* should take these decisions and *how* in terms of the procedures and processes governing them.

On the *who* question, should it be politicians, managers, doctors, the public or some combination of these groups who should be responsible for taking decisions about who to offer care to and whom to deny it? And, if so, how should they be engaged in the process and held to account for their actions? How explicit should the process be in contrast to the emphasis on implicit, by which is usually (and misleadingly) meant covert, decision-making? What information or evidence should be available to decision-makers – whoever they are – and how, if at all, will they be equipped to interpret it? Moreover, does it exist anyway given that a substantial amount of clinical care has not been evaluated for its impact on health? These and other questions lead to the second big question: *how* to ration health care. The *how* question gives rise to a number of issues: in particular, and depending on the outcome to the first question, what procedures should be followed to ensure that decisions are taken responsibly and transparently, and at what level in the hierarchy of decision-making should they operate: macro (national), meso (local) or micro (doctor–patient) levels or at a mix of levels?

Should rationing be explicit or implicit?

The book is primarily concerned with these types of question in the context of the British NHS, especially in its post-1991 reform phase when rationing took on a whole new meaning as a result of the introduction of a purchaser–provider relationship and the related notions of an internal market operating according to competitive principles. Whereas the former, i.e. pre-1991, integrated structure of planning and provision allowed rationing decisions to be made implicitly by health authorities and clinicians acting beyond the public gaze, the market-style changes with their emphasis on separating purchasing and providing responsibilities on the one hand, and on giving an active voice to users on the other, have resulted in rationing being regarded as an activity which is much more explicit and open to scrutiny. In a democracy, it is argued, this must be a desirable development and wholly in keeping with the approach to participatory democracy favoured by many political reformers who see the former implicit system as deficient in every way but especially in its perpetuation of an outmoded, élitist and paternalistic system of decision-making in which users were to remain passive recipients of whatever the professionals thought was best for them.

A key theme of the book is the debate between those who subscribe to the view that rationing should be explicit, and given a national lead by the government, and those who take a rather more subtle and less naïve view of how health care is practised and who believe that implicit rationing is the best policy option – bearing in mind that however the subject is viewed there is no perfect or right answer.

This author has already nailed his colours to the mast and declared his position as a firm believer in implicit rationing (Hunter 1993a; 1995a). The position is based on pragmatism and *realpolitik*. While explicit rationing may be intellectually irrefutable, and the rational response to adopt in a perfect world, the reality is not conducive to the serious adoption of such a stance. The position will be elaborated as the book unfolds. Least it be thought that those who remain wedded to implicit rationing are an élitist band of diehard reactionaries who possess a somewhat romanticized and paternalistic view of doctors and medical power on the one hand, and a dismissive view of patient power or consumerism on the other, nothing could be further from the truth. The issue is not whether change is required in current practice – it is – but rather on the kind of change and where and how it is needed and should be implemented. This is a very difficult set of issues – much more so than calling (naïvely and simplistically in my view) for a national, explicit response which might take the form of either a menu or list of those procedures which are to be included in the NHS and those which are not, or a set of guiding principles for decision-makers to use which are likely to be so general and non-specific as to be virtually meaningless. Hence the term adopted to describe the approach I favour – 'muddling through elegantly' (Hunter 1993a) – which will be unpacked in Chapter 6. The 'elegantly' is important because it signals that merely muddling through is not sufficient but is in need of modification and improvement. However, it also acknowledges and accepts that some decisions are so difficult, and 'unwinnable' in Heclo's (1975) term, that muddling through is not only the most likely option to be adopted in practice but also the most realistic and pragmatic. Rather than be rejected it should be positively embraced.

It needs to be emphasized that while rationing clearly raises many political and ethical issues with which politicians, managers and practitioners are almost daily struggling to come to terms, if we are honest and realistic then some of these issues will simply not be confronted because they cannot be. In the cut and thrust of politics they will quite simply be fudged. There may be a pretence cunningly fashioned to suggest that they are being, or have been, addressed but this will only mislead by deception and connivance. Yet a policy response based on fudge may be considered, and prove to be, a perfectly reasonable, even rational, response if policy stasis or gridlock is not to occur.

A central theme of this book is that the currently fashionable managerialist notions of user empowerment, explicitness and transparency, and the desire for constantly probing, tinkering with, and subjecting to bureaucratic scrutiny, the delicate workings and operating procedures which have evolved over decades about determining how choices in health care are made, may actually be counter-productive or rapidly in danger of becoming so. Far from helping society to function better and in a more mature manner, such forensic behaviour may be creating a set of circumstances in which it becomes ever more difficult to transact the business sensibly in a given policy sphere. Far from improving the efficiency and effectiveness of practice and its impact – the ostensible aims of the new managerialism – the supreme policy paradox must be that these desirable and laudable goals will be denied reformers.

The globalization of new public management

These musings may seem to divert us from the core purpose of this book, which is to shed light and understanding on the vexed issue of rationing health care. But it would be a mistake to think so. The matters just touched on go to the heart of why rationing has become a major policy puzzle for all those engaged in the health-care 'industry', as it is commonly known. Moreover, the issue of rationing cannot be seen in isolation from the wider changes taking place not only in the health-policy landscape but also beyond in terms of the implications of what has been termed the 'new public management' (Hood 1991), and the developments derived from it. All these issues and developments are inextricably linked and therefore a broad sweep across the public policy landscape, and its management, is presented in order to provide a proper context for examining rationing in health care.

A final key dimension of the approach adopted to the subject of rationing health care is its international focus. Just as health-care reform has not been confined to the UK, nor has the issue of rationing. The governments of countries as different as the US, New Zealand, Sweden and The Netherlands, to name only a few, have all been exercised by attempts to square the circle of demand outstripping supply. The various solutions adopted (or not) are described and reviewed in Chapter 5, and the lessons for policy extracted, but perhaps a more interesting question at this point is why countries with such different cultures, political systems and health-care services are all facing a common set of policy puzzles to which none has so far found an acceptable response. Are countries converging? And if so, why should this convergence be happening at roughly the same time? An even more interesting question might be why there is convergence at all when many of the problems to which health-care reform is a response appear to be stubbornly resistant to all known solutions?

There is unlikely to be a monocausal explanation for any of these questions. James and Manning (1996) link this global activity to the new public management. They see it as an example of 'globalization' processes in public management which themselves have their roots in a set of pressures common across countries. Three pressures in particular are most acute: fiscal pressure (leading to a search for cost-containment measures in policy areas like health care), citizen pressure (resulting in more assertive and demanding citizens acting as consumers who wish to see rapid improvements in public services), and the international promotion of reform ideas. This last pressure is particularly intriguing. As James and Manning (1996: 144) describe the phenomenon: 'international management consultancy firms and public management organisations present the new forms to public managers as best practice'. Some of these firms have offices in more than 100 countries and provide a similar 'package' to different countries, thus spreading the new management concepts rapidly and with a degree of consistency previously unattainable. All these efforts are informed by a market-based ideology in which private sector practice is seen to be superior and as providing a model for the transformation of allegedly underperforming, low-quality public services and public sector management.

When these ideas are harnessed to the international community of management consultancies, which are no respectors of national boundaries, it is easy to see how an international policy culture of public sector management reform has developed. As a consequence, what Rose (1993) terms 'lesson-drawing' is given a significant boost at a global level. Ideas and new forms of tackling policy problems and delivering care are communicated much more rapidly. If the globe is not converging then it is certainly contracting in terms of the transmission of, and access to, information especially when filtered through conduits like management consultancies. In fact, the practices adopted to rationing health care are divergent at this stage rather than convergent and therefore offer rich opportunities for lesson-drawing in public policy.

The argument so far

To summarize the discussion so far, this book is concerned with taking an approach to rationing health care which seeks to place the issue in its wider political and economic context before looking at the specific managerial and professional issues that are uppermost in any discussion of rationing principally in the UK but also elsewhere. Therefore, it becomes necessary to go back a stage and investigate some of the value-based and ethical concerns which underpin the design and direction of health-care systems in a given country. This in turn leads to a consideration of the twin concepts of need and demand and their application in a particular system before moving on to consider matters like the coverage of health care, its funding basis and management. It is then necessary to consider whether in fact rationing is inevitable or not or whether it is a tactical device on the part of those who take the view that the NHS cannot cope with the demands on it and that its political masters must therefore decide, by which they mean 'come clean', on what the NHS can do and what people must either forego or seek privately.

A variant of this view is that rationing is simply an excuse for not confronting powerful clinical vested interests, whose activities do not contribute to health gain, in order to reallocate finite resources from ineffective to effective procedures. Were this to be done rigorously, and in the context of existing as well as new medical developments, then sufficient resources would exist to meet all needs (and possibly demands) placed upon them thereby making rationing unnecessary or redundant. The sceptics (or realists) are less convinced by such seemingly persuasive and seductive logic. They do not believe the evidence will ever be sufficiently unequivocal or uncontested to allow many (if any) firm decisions to be made according to it. Nor do they believe that even where, or if, such evidence existed it would be sufficient to result in clinicians modifying their behaviour. They concede some useful progress may be possible but that it is likely to be marginal and modest and therefore most unlikely to remove the need for rationing in some form.

If rationing as a policy problem is seen to be an inevitable, if regrettable, fact of organizational life and to grow out of a common set of pressures, principally around cost containment and a more demanding citizenry, then the next aspect of the issue to consider is the extent to which it should be regarded as an explicit or implicit process and the consequences of adopting one or other approach. International experience can be valuable in illuminating what can all too easily become a narrow, insular discussion conducted locally if not nationally. Rationing is one of those areas notable for its policy divergence as countries are still at the stage of experimenting with new forms rather than mimicking or aping those which appear to work well. If a workable solution is found then it is likely that a degree of policy convergence will occur. But we are still some way from that state of affairs.

Rationing health care is, then, an issue of growing concern and interest to all those engaged in this activity whether as policy-makers, practitioners or recipients. But this is not to argue that it is a new problem. Far from it. Rationing is as old as the NHS – indeed, older. What has changed, or to be more precise what many wish to see changed, is the degree to which rationing should remain implicit or should become explicit. Those who argue in favour of rationing becoming explicit cite the 1991 NHS reforms as heralding a significant shift in policy.

Somewhere between the paternalists who wish the *status quo* to continue unchanged on the one hand and advocates of citizen power on the other is a third group who might be labelled realists. They take the view that the implicit system of rationing has many advantages and that we overthrow it at our peril. Being explicit may not always be preferable or an improvement on what went before. But this same group also acknowledges the need to equalize the power balance between professionals and users respectively where the latter are often unable for a variety of reasons to get their own views across or to be seen as genuine co-partners or co-producers in their own health. This book falls into this third category.

The approach

The book is not based on original, primary research examining the issue of health-care rationing. It draws heavily on secondary sources of some relevance to rationing which derive from work conducted by the author and others. The principal source of evidence, however, is the author himself who has been observing, analysing and writing about health policy for almost 20 years and has been interested in the specific issue of rationing health care for the past five years, writing fairly extensively about it over this period either solo or with colleagues. The book provides a timely opportunity to expand on these earlier writings, to update the thinking behind them, and to put them within an international comparative context. Although I have adopted a clearly articulated position about the rationing debate in the UK, and am extremely sceptical of the policy options favoured by those who wish to see greater public involvement and more overt central government leadership in rationing, the book is certainly not to be read as a polemical tract. Nor is it intended to be one. It endeavours to set out the various arguments and their respective pros and cons fairly and with equanimity in order to allow the reader to judge for themselves the balance of opinions between the competing views and to arrive at their own conclusions. At the same time, academic detachment does not intrude to the extent that punches are pulled. There is a clearly articulated position which lies at the core of the book: namely, that though imperfect, the current approach to rationing may be a good deal less so than any of the alternative approaches being proposed.

There are two reasons for writing this book. First, no single text currently available seeks to deal with the subject in such a wide-ranging way or in a format which aims to bring together different viewpoints: namely, those of politicians, managers, practitioners and the public. Nor is there a text which tries to do this within an international context or framework. Although most of the material reviewed in subsequent chapters is of a secondary nature that is accessible separately in published form, the strength of its treatment here is the bringing together of a mass of disparate material within a single volume. Hopefully, this will be of considerable value to students, interested members of the public who may also be non-executive directors on health authorities and trust boards, and busy managers with no time to sift (or should it be surf in these days of the Internet?) through the literature. While no claim is made to be comprehensive in reviewing the literature, the main arguments are examined.

The second reason for writing the book has already been alluded to. In my opinion, a great deal of the writing and commentary on the rationing issue in the UK is woefully inadequate and lacking depth or substance. It is slight, superficial, ill-informed and has done a grave disservice to anyone genuinely seeking understanding and illumination of a complex policy puzzle. Rationing health care offers no easy solutions and to imply or pretend there are, as many commentators and analysts do, possibly unwittingly, is quite misleading and simply unacceptable. There may be no difficult solutions either since they may be regarded as unacceptable or intolerable. This book, therefore, aims to restore a sense of balance to the proceedings. Its starting point in achieving its mission is to acknowledge that rationing health care is not a neutral, objective value-free activity. Rather, it is intensely political and value-laden. Rationing goes to the heart of what the NHS stands for in terms of its founding principles, notably the provision of comprehensive health care for all those in need of it that is largely free at the point of use. It also exposes the various stakeholder interests in health care and the power relations between them. Finally, it offers insights into the minds of ministers who are keen simultaneously to centralize and decentralize responsibility in those areas where it suits them to adopt one strategy in preference to the other. In Rudolf Klein's famous observation, governments centralize credit and diffuse blame. Since no astute minister or right-thinking politician could conceive of any credit being forthcoming from centralizing responsibility for rationing health care, it only makes sense to devolve responsibility for it to the agents of ministers: namely, health authorities and trust boards. How they cope with the task, or more likely do not cope with it, is therefore of greater interest than that associated with what ministers should or should not do. And who can blame ministers for not wishing to get involved? They of all people are only too well aware of the dilemmas and pitfalls arising from rationing especially when it becomes explicit. They embrace it at their peril.

Structure of book

The remainder of the book falls into five chapters. Chapter 2 is concerned with defining terms. The use of language is important because it conveys, intentionally or unintentionally, positive or negative signals and messages. It is of particular interest to note that the term 'rationing' is a fairly recent entry into the NHS lexicon, only becoming part of common currency in the years since the 1991 NHS changes. Up until then terms like 'choice' and 'priority setting' were more commonly used. Most obviously, these did not carry pejorative overtones of scarcity or denial or withdrawal of treatment. The terms used to describe the setting of priorities are therefore important in establishing both the substance and the tone of public debate. This chapter reviews such matters and also the implied assumption that whereas priority-setting is concerned with whole groups and populations, rationing is more directed to individuals and to the treatment offered or denied them. Just as with the NHS changes as a whole, at the core of the debate about rationing is a tension between the needs of the individual versus those of the collective or community. If we were to simplify and caricature the distinction, the NHS has traditionally put the interests of the collective before those of the individual. The 1991 NHS changes sought to give a higher priority to the needs of the individual in keeping with market mechanisms and a consumer culture. Rationing, therefore, is a key concept in the lexicon of health-care markets and their operation and cannot readily be divorced from them.

Part Two reviews the health-care rationing debate in the UK. In Chapter 3, the nature of the health-care rationing debate in the UK as it has evolved since the 1991 NHS changes is described. The chapter explores the reasons for rationing becoming a major public policy issue in the NHS notwithstanding government protestations, largely well founded, that additional resources have been allocated to the NHS, even if they still fall short of what many inside and outside the NHS believe is required. The chapter considers the impact so far of the internal market and its implications for explicit, in place of implicit, rationing. A difficulty here lies in the absence of sound independent evaluation of the 1991 NHS changes.

Chapter 4 considers the issue of whether rationing should be a national or local matter and assesses the arguments on both sides. It also reviews the move towards evidence-based medicine and documents the shift towards consumer empowerment and a growing awareness of a rights-based approach to health care. These developments have fuelled the rationing debate and demands for it to be more explicit and open to public scrutiny.

Part Three turns to the international context and prospects for the future. A variety of practices and instruments are being employed, or are under active consideration, to aid the rationing task in many countries and some of the more developed among these are appraised in Chapter 5. Probably Oregon is the most famous and most written-about approach but there are others. Countries everywhere are talking about, and some are experimenting with, various options. A few countries have tried, largely unsuccessfully, to find solutions to the rationing dilemma and put it on a more rational basis – such as the search for a basic basket of services or a set of core services or a guaranteed entitlement to health care. For the most part, these efforts have been disappointing and found wanting.

The final chapter – Chapter 6 – on issues and prospects examines the rationing debate in the light of the preceding chapters and endeavours to draw some conclusions from it. These form the basis of an examination of options for addressing some of the dilemmas arising from rationing, in particular the extent to which it should be explicit and involve the public in determining priorities. This chapter explores further my views on what the nature of the problem is and how it might be tackled. There are no right or perfect answers when it comes to resolving the rationing dilemma, although some may be more acceptable and achievable than others.

By the end of the book, it is hoped that the reader will be better informed about the subject of rationing health care, have had their assumptions or prejudices challenged, or at least subjected to searching scrutiny, and have acquired a deeper appreciation of how difficult, complex and intensely political the subject is. If the book achieves all this, or even gets close to doing so, then its purpose will have been amply served.

CHAPTER 2

Defining terms

Introduction

'Rationing' is a term with pejorative overtones. Since the 1991 NHS changes it has become a key word in the unofficial lexicon of health policy. Officially, rather like 'health inequalities', the word is outlawed and successive Secretaries of State have refused to grace it with their approval. They prefer to use the terms 'priority-setting' and 'making choices'. Indeed, until the 1991 changes, these terms were in common currency in official policy statements and plans. 'Priority-setting' is viewed as a term which makes rationing 'sound a little less grim, and a little more scientific, than in fact it is' (Loughlin 1996: 146). Rationing is associated with limited supply. The word is linked to the notion of sacrifice and to emergency or exceptional situations where resources are limited, such as wartime rations.

Words are important because the terms used to define phenomena reveal much about the processes and activities they seek to describe or, conversely, obscure or conceal. They also illustrate the broader state of a policy field, like health, and how it is perceived both by the politicians who shape it and by the public who are its recipients and also, hopefully, its beneficiaries. Given the NHS's popularity with the public, politicians tread warily when it comes to matters which might be politically damaging. The 1991 NHS changes have not been at all popular with the public who, for the most part, probably do not fully understand them in any case. But, whatever the reasons for their lack of popularity, the changes led the public to be even more suspicious of a government which was seen to be ideologically opposed to the very concept of the NHS despite repeated assurances and protestations to the contrary. No doubt such reactions contributed to the defeat of the Conservative government in May 1997. The use of the term 'rationing' cannot therefore be divorced from the overall package of NHS changes introduced in 1991 with their emphasis on competitive market-style approaches, including a focus on responding more sensitively to user preferences. These developments were in sharp contrast to earlier reforms in the health service through the 1970s and 1980s which had largely been confined to structural and managerial concerns but within a firmly collectivist public service framework. The adoption of business principles, private sector management practices and a consumerist focus did not begin to take a grip until the arrival of general management in the early 1980s which paved the way for the 1991 changes. These later developments, which provide the context for the current debates on rationing, are the subject of Chapter 3. This current chapter is concerned with reviewing notions about what constitutes rationing, and the background to its emergence in the 1990s as an issue high on the health-policy agenda with the shift from the language of priority-setting to that of rationing.

The problem

The problem of allocating scarce resources in health care has always existed, and not just in the UK. It has become a truism to assert that setting priorities and choosing where and how to invest resources are unavoidable political and management tasks. As health economists are forever reminding us, resources have been and are likely always to be scarce and it will never be possible to meet all health needs (Mooney *et al.* 1992). But not all policy analysts or philosophers accept that rationing is inevitable or that we should embrace it wholeheartedly, if not enthusiastically, as an awkward fact of life in a public service seeking to match growing need (or is it demand?) with static or diminishing resources. For instance, Mullen (1995), reviewing arguments which challenge the grim inevitability of rationing, notes the rather pessimistic and defeatist thread running through the arguments of those who, in Califano's (1992) words, 'seem bent on elevating health care rationing to a national policy'. 'Rationing,' he states, 'is not a solution to the problems we face, it is a capitulation of despair.'

Mullen (1995) considers the claims of those who question the whole notion of rationing and who see it as a diversion from the real problem of the funding and delivery of care. In a similar vein, but writing from a philosophical perspective, Loughlin (1996: 147) takes to task health economists and others who profess to have solutions to problems like establishing priorities and whose 'toxic effect' is to obscure 'the monstrous irrationality and barbarity' of modern society. He continues: 'the assumption that there must be a defensible, determinate answer to questions about who should be allowed to suffer and die, is false' (1995: 155). More fundamentally, Loughlin is critical of the very nature of the narrow parameters within which the rationing debate is being conducted. By definition these are not givens or objective phenomena, but are politically determined.

Unwillingness to think about radical changes in the organisation of social reality when trying to determine what is right or best, reflects not realism but the unwillingness to admit any major differences between the way the world is and how it ought to be. It suggests the disposition to believe that the world is just about right as it is, that the social background to health service policy is morally uncontroversial.

(Loughlin 1996: 155)

There is also the matter of how rational rationing can be when society may not in fact be rational (Loughlin 1996). Perhaps the assumptions we make about the nature of society are less rational than we like to believe. If so, what grounds are there for believing that any explicit rationing system either can or should succeed?

More prosaically, most of those who challenge the prevailing orthodoxy that need is infinite (Frankel 1991; Roberts *et al.* 1995) believe there may be no need to ration those interventions of proven effectiveness. In their view, the denial of non-effective treatment does not constitute rationing which is presumably why ministers refuse to use the term and prefer instead to speak in enthusiastic terms of the NHS research and development strategy, introduced in 1991, and its promise of evidence-based medicine (or health care) and clinical effectiveness. Whether such optimism is justified is assessed in Chapter 4. Certainly it is challenged by many who think that it is already possible to carry out more procedures of demonstrable effectiveness than there are resources to fund them (Healthcare 2000 1995). However, the point here is that whatever terminology is used, making choices to do more or less of something, or not to do it at all, is a feature of all health-care systems. Even at its most sophisticated and precise, it is doubtful if the knowledge-base of clinical decision-making will be able to remove entirely the need for choices between equally needed and effective treatments. The problem of setting priorities raises some of the most difficult moral questions facing society today – not only in the UK but globally. Although frequently portrayed as such, the issues are not primarily technical but political.

The political problem can be simply expressed: the *demand*, if not need, for health care seems likely to forever outstrip supply. Continuous advances in medicine have heightened popular expectations of health and of what health-care services can do to alleviate suffering. In short, health-care services, and those who provide them, are victims of their own success. Compounding the policy dilemma is the erroneous, though widely held, perception that medical care equals health. Although empirically wrong – more available medical care does not equal better health – politicians who take this view are vulnerable when confronted by a public who assume such heresy betrays a hidden agenda based on withholding necessary resources, rationing health care and allowing the health of the population to deteriorate. It is not a position any politician intent on furthering or just maintaining their political career is likely to occupy, however convinced they may be privately of the public's folly in believing that medical care and improved health are inseparable.

The best estimates are that health services affect about 10 per cent of the usual indices for measuring health: infant mortality, absences through sickness and adult mortality. The remaining 90 per cent are determined by factors over which doctors have little or no control: individual lifestyle, social conditions and the physical environment. As

Wildavsky (1979) observes, 'No one is saying that medicine is good for nothing, only that it is not good for everything.'

Wildavsky's thesis that we are 'doing better but feeling worse' is based on the evidence of history that past successes lead to future failures. Most pressure on health-care (including social-care) systems comes from long-term chronic disabling conditions as the easier ills have by and large been dealt with (although as WHO has warned many of the infectious diseases once thought conquered, like tuberculosis, diphtheria and malaria, are making an alarming comeback).

But just as there is no free lunch, as economists are fond of telling us, there is no free health care – even if it is available to all free at the point of use. Choices have to be made and rationing takes place. It can occur by time (waiting lists, times), by distance (people who live further from facilities use them less that those who live closer to them), by complexity (bureaucratic procedures, rules, regulations and forms, repeated visits), by space (limiting the number of beds and clinical staff available), or by any or all of these methods in combination (see further below).

Even when health-care services experience steady year-on-year growth, as the NHS enjoyed during the 1980s and early 1990s, dissatisfaction with services persists. There never seems to be enough to do everything that is possible or desirable. Some see this as a structural, systemic problem as far as the NHS is concerned. A former Minister of State for Health, Enoch Powell, wrote in 1966:

One of the most striking features of the NHS is the continual, deafening chorus of complaint which rises day and night from every part of it, a chorus only interrupted when someone suggests that a different system altogether might be preferable, which would involve the money coming from some less (literally) palpable source.

(Powell 1966: 16)

Powell noted the endemic wish on the part of health-care professionals to denigrate services in the hope of winning additional resources. To sing the praises of the NHS risked at best standing still in resource terms or at worst actually losing resources to possibly 'less deserving' causes.

But if the demand for health care, whether real or artificial, reasonable or unreasonable, is a major political problem, the other side of the equation – supply – is a key component of it. As demand grows, supply does too, although usually lagging some way behind. A feature of supply-side behaviour is supplier-induced demand whereby new developments, drugs and treatments create a demand (often with the active encouragement of enthusiastic doctors perhaps egged on by pharmaceutical companies and other 'health industry' interests) where none previously existed. This demand might arise regardless of whether the treatment or drug has been adequately evaluated for its cost-effectiveness (Freemantle 1995). But whatever the source of the demand for care, the chief problem is the increasing cost of meeting it. With the demise of most infectious diseases, despite the recurrence of some which were thought to have been eradicated, the high cost of care comes from the acute and chronic long-term care sectors which are heavy consumers of drugs, tests and, most expensive of all, labour.

Given the pressures and realities noted above, it is hardly surprising that the NHS was founded on a fallacy: that there was a finite amount of ill-health in the population which, once removed, would result in the maintenance of health and the provision of health care becoming cheaper as the need for it dropped off. What has happened is that success in health care has resulted in people living longer potentially to be ill more often and therefore consume more resources which themselves are not unlimited. At the same time, medicine does not stand still and new technologies and treatments are constantly appearing although *a priori* there is no reason why these need always cost more money, as is often assumed, if they are able to procure savings in the delivery of care.

So, given how politicians and public conceive of the issue, rationing, priority-setting, making choices, or whatever term is preferred, is inevitable at least to *some* degree (precisely to what degree will depend on the particular health-care system in question and the level of funding it enjoys) – it is an endemic feature of *all* health-care systems regardless of their financing and organization. Both market and administrative systems have been compelled to ration. The key differences lie in the mechanism(s) used and the impact on the public and not in the fact of rationing itself. The 1979 Royal Commission on the NHS asserted that 'the capacity of health services to absorb resources is almost unlimited. Choices have therefore to be made about the use of available funds and priorities have to be set. The more pressure there is on resources, the more important it is to get the priorities clear' (Royal Commission on the NHS 1979, note 9, para. 6.1).

Having reviewed the arguments which subscribe to the prevailing orthodoxy that rationing is inevitable (and interestingly those of this persuasion also insist that rationing be explicit and public, rather than remain implicit and the preserve of doctors, and that 'hard choices' are needed), as well as those which challenge this 'defeatism' on the grounds that it represents a monumental failure to address deeper failings in our social and political structures, it is necessary to be a bit more precise about some key features of priority-setting and rationing. In particular, how are these terms defined? Are the differences between them important and of more than semantical interest? What mechanisms are there for rationing? What are its dimensions? At what levels does it operate, and who should do it?

Defining terms: priority-setting and rationing

The terms 'priority-setting' and 'rationing' are both used, often interchangeably, in deliberations about the allocation of resources. It is sometimes implied that there is a distinction to be made between the two and that one is a positive process while the other is negative (or defeatist). For example, priority-setting is about deciding what the NHS should provide while rationing is about deciding what the NHS should not provide, or to whom treatment should be denied (BMA 1995a). In practice, this distinction does not survive close scrutiny as it is implicit when setting priorities within tight budgets that some services of lower priority will not be available. Denial, if not scarcity, is therefore a feature of both priority-setting and rationing.

Rationing (and priority-setting) can be defined in a variety of ways. In its evidence to the House of Commons Health Committee (1995b), the Association of CHCs for England and Wales identified three distinct forms of rationing:

- withdrawal of the NHS from a particular type of service for treatment (e.g. 'cosmetic' operations, the treatment of infertility, long-term care of the elderly)
- explicit and regular attempts to define how much of which services should be provided and moving resources between services
- restricting access to a service by reference to the characteristics of prospective patients, e.g. their age, personal lifestyle (whether they smoke, take drugs, are heavy drinkers and so on).

We consider each of these forms in the next section.

Mechanisms for priority-setting and rationing

Rationing can and does occur commonly through a number of devices or mechanisms. Some were listed earlier. These and others can be grouped under five headings as set out in Box 2.1. A particularly problematic form of rationing both ethically and in policy terms concerns lifestyle factors. These can manifest themselves in any or all of the mechanisms just listed. Establishing the criteria employed in treatment decisions and how decisions on treatment are made is difficult. As Aaron and Schwartz observe in their comparative study of rationing in the USA and Britain, 'few of the criteria for rejection are explicitly stated. Age, for example, is not officially identified as an obstacle to treatment' (Aaron and Schwartz 1984: 37). Yet there is very clear evidence which appears regularly that age is a major factor in determining whether treatment is sanctioned or denied. Grimley Evans (1993: 203) argues that 'The use of health resources by older age groups may have been kept inappropriately low through covert age discrimination that should be abolished.' The use of age as a criterion for rationing health care is based on a simple proposition: limits on health care for elderly people are justifiable because each citizen, throughout a lifetime, would benefit if funds now used to extend life at its end were redirected to earlier stages of life. Such a principle would place a higher premium on communalism than on individualism. Death would be accepted at the end of a natural life span or 'fair innings'.

Box 2.1   Rationing mechanisms

- *Deterrence*. Rationing can occur by obstructing the demands for health care through mechanisms such as user co-payments (e.g. prescription and dental charges) or the inconvenient location of services and facilities which cuts down on their use.

- *Delay*. Waiting lists (and times) are a good example of delay, functioning as a holding area to buffer excess demand.

- *Deflection*. The use of GPs as gatekeepers to secondary care to deflect demand for secondary care and channel it into primary care. GPs may also deflect the demand for health services altogether by shifting it to social services and therefore on to another agency's budget. Giving patients more information about treatments, outcomes and side-effects may also have this effect as people may choose not to proceed with a particular operation or treatment.

- *Dilution*. Health-care demand can be diluted by reducing the amount of service offered, e.g. the use of fewer tests or attendances, or its quality, e.g. the use of cheaper drugs. Clinical freedom, as was mentioned earlier, may also serve as a means of dilution whereby decisions not to treat are couched in terms of clinical decisions thereby obscuring what are, in effect, rationing decisions.

- *Denial*. The exclusion of services from the NHS or their denial to individual patients or groups of patients (e.g. IVF services, tattoo removal).

Source: Harrison and Hunter (1994: 25–30).

Evidence of age discrimination exists for the access of older people to coronary care and thrombolysis (Grimley Evans 1993) as well as to treatment for end-stage renal failure. There is also a view that age discrimination could arise if purchasing authorities in the NHS negotiate separate contracts for different age groups especially if resource pressures continue to exist. These will, or could, encourage practitioners to inhibit the access of older patients to expensive but beneficial specialist care. While age discrimination does not officially exist, it clearly occurs in practice. Rather than physiological assessment alone being the criterion determining access, many practitioners employ an arbitrary age cut-off. Many health economists, notably Callahan (1987) in the USA and Williams (1997) in the UK, adopt a similar approach but advocate the need for explicitness and for there to be a broad social consensus governing decision-making. Their position is unequivocally and aggressively utilitarian in outlook and is based on older people having had 'a fair innings' and it being children who can most benefit in cost-effectiveness terms from the consumption of health care.

But geriatricians and social gerontologists dispute this line of argument not only on social justice grounds but because ageing itself is a dynamic process. Grimley Evans (1993: 204) again:

It is facile to assume that increased longevity will inevitably lead to increased numbers of people reaching ages at which average health costs rise. The data suggest that the longer one delays the onset of disabling disease the shorter the average period of survival in a disabled state.

In response to health economists' quality-of-life methodology, Grimley Evans counters:

Total costs per life year may therefore not correlate directly with average life expectancy. The framework within which economic analyses of this kind have to be made needs to be defined ideologically. Most citizens . . . would regard prevention of disabling diseases and prolongation of healthy life as good things and, from society's point of view, a good investment.

At root, age discrimination in accessing health care appears to have more to do with the prevalence of a focus on youth combined with negative stereotypes of which older age groups are still the victims. Imagery like 'the burden of ageing' and 'the rising tide of the elderly' is commonplace in the media. Positive views of ageing would be unlikely to be reflected in rationing decisions currently based on age.

Age is not the only criterion for selecting patients for treatment but it is the most readily applied. Klein, Day and Redmayne (1996: 87) suggest this is because 'it provides an automatic pilot for doctors, so simplifying the perplexities, and avoiding the agonies, of choosing between different lives'.

While age is clearly a rationing criterion in respect of kidney failure, it is not the only reason why a patient may be rejected (Aaron and Schwartz 1984). Vascular complications and other medical diseases, physical handicaps and mental illness are also common reasons for rejection. However, the criteria vary widely from locality to locality with no standard approach in operation.

The capacity of a patient to benefit from treatment, or the probability that they will, is another common rationing criterion and one preferred by those opposed to rationing by age (Levinsky 1990). For instance, a doctor may decide not to operate on a patient with a heart problem if that person is also a heavy smoker. The doctor will argue in their own defence that this does not constitute a moral judgement on that person's lifestyle or habits but is a decision reached on clinical grounds. So, even if a patient needs treatment and is not subject to an age cut-off, they might be vulnerable to a criterion of appropriateness or capacity to benefit. Smoking is commonly cited because patients who smoke heavily spend longer in hospital and have poorer results.

There are two difficulties with this principle which on the surface seems reasonable enough. First, there is the issue of judgement. Though an essential, and to some extent desirable, feature of professional practice, doctors do vary in the judgements they make. This is inevitable and is both the strength and weakness of judgement as a decision criterion. Moreover, and this is where the second difficulty arises, it is very easy for denial of treatment on capacity to benefit grounds to slide into denial on rather more suspect moral grounds whereby patients who smoke heavily are seen as less deserving and as getting their 'just deserts'. And it is not only smoking but alcohol and substance misuse more generally which is vulnerable to decisions being taken on moral rather than clinical grounds. For instance, it was reported at an inquiry in January 1997 that doctors at a Scottish hospital refused to perform a liver transplant on a dying girl because she had experimented with drugs. The girl died of acute liver failure after taking ecstasy at a party. Her mother told the inquiry that doctors had refused treatment 'on moral grounds, because to give her the £60 000 operation would mean denying a healthier person' (*The Times* 1997: 1). The inquiry found in favour of the doctor and of the clinical case for withholding treatment. Although doctors are forbidden to allow moral judgements to enter into their decision-making, it is in practice sometimes difficult to disentangle these from what can be presented as clinical judgements based on capacity to benefit.

But views are divided on this point. If clinical judgement and trust between doctor and patient are seen as two principal pillars of what a caring professional regards as the essence of professionalism and as being at the centre of their craft, then judgements based on a patient's capacity to benefit from treatment and on the likely burdensome consequences of treatment for the patient (both evident in the Child B case) are ethically defensible in principle, fallible though they may be (Gormally 1996). The need is for a better understanding of clinical decision-making.

In their study of cardiac surgery and its availability to different patients, Hughes and Griffiths (1996: 173) examine the decision-making process and its claim to be based on 'purely technical judgements, devoid of moral or social content'. In practice, the researchers found that doctors moved between 'technical' and 'social' discourse frames to make sense of patient histories. 'Far from remaining exclusively within a neutral medico-technical discourse, doctors construct arguments and counter-arguments that closely resemble the standpoints in the wider public debate on rationing and deservingness' (Hughes and Griffiths 1996). The content of medical work is therefore a complex mix of clinical factors, effectiveness of resource use and policing lifestyle. Technical and social assessments become interwoven, thus giving the lie to the assumption that medical practice is a technical, value-free activity. While those who are concerned about this practice advocate explicit rationing as a way of exposing and holding to account the making of moral judgements, there is no reason to believe that explicit rationing would in fact be any more rational. As Hughes and Griffiths (1996: 172) state, 'It is perfectly possible for doctors to act according to their perceptions of deservingness, while accounting for their actions in terms of medical benefit.' At a time of tighter resource pressures, clinical grounds are not in themselves sufficient to decide who should receive treatment. Therefore, moral concerns come into play. This combination of pressures seemed to lie at the centre of the case cited above of the girl who had taken ecstasy and was denied a liver transplant.

Much of the criticism of implicit rationing derives from the dubious and covert moral practices which underlie much medical decision-making and account for much of the variation in medical practice. But there is an important distinction to be made between the terms 'implicit' and 'covert'. They are not interchangeable although they are often treated as such. Implicit decision-making, which is confined to the parties directly involved, may be an entirely open, equally balanced and appropriate process. Covert decision-making, on the other hand, is suggestive of an altogether more secretive process in which information is deliberately withheld and not shared by all the parties directly involved.

Dimensions and levels of priority-setting and of rationing

Dimensions

Klein (1992a) has suggested that rationing has four dimensions:

- decisions about the allocation of resources to broad sectors or client groups (e.g. elderly, mentally ill, antenatal care, cancer and so on)
- decisions about the allocation of resources to specific interventions and forms of treatment
- decisions about how to prioritize access to treatment between different patients
- decisions about how much to invest in individual patients once access has been achieved.

There is a fifth dimension which is concerned with decisions at central government level about how much to allocate to health care as against competing demands on public resources such as education, social security, defence and so on. But our chief area of interest is in what happens to the slice of the cake that is allocated to the NHS and how it is further subdivided.

Levels

The four dimensions of rationing listed above can be linked to levels in the structure of the NHS and responsibilities for them assigned accordingly. Within the current NHS structure, the first two dimensions would be the responsibility of macro (central government: DoH and NHS Executive) and meso (health authorities) levels respectively, while the second two would be the responsibility of doctors operating at the micro level. An additional responsibility for the macro level, as already mentioned, is to decide the proportion of public expenditure which should be devoted to the NHS as opposed to other competing demands. Levels of rationing become important when considering *who* should ration or set priorities. It is this question which has prompted the most intense and heated debate on the subject. We return to it in Chapter 4.

In his discussion on rational rationing or reasonable rationing, Gormally (1996: 3) concentrates on the first two levels – the split of the health authority's budget between care groups and sectors of health

care, and decisions about the allocation of resources to specific interventions and treatments – since he has 'rather less confidence in the
ethics or morality . . . of certain approaches to decision-making' at these
levels. He believes the problem arises from the government's refusal to
set a framework of principles for priority-setting with the result that
local managers 'often find themselves floundering' (Gormally 1996: 3).
A rather curious assumption perhaps is that *a priori* central government
would flounder less which seems to fly in the face of actual experience.
But let this seeming aberration not detain or divert us here. We return
to it in the final chapter.

Gormally is critical of the various public consultation exercises that
have been carried out because the outputs from them are heavily con-
tingent on what has gone into them. But his main criticism is that most,
if not all, health authorities are motivated by a strong concern for efficiency with, possibly, a concern for equity lurking somewhere in the
background if we are lucky, although there is a lack of clarity about
what precisely is required in respect of equitable health care priority-
setting. All this leads Gormally to bemoan the absence of an adequate
framework for explicit rationing. In his opinion, other countries do it
better – notably the Dutch (see further Chapter 5).

In devising a framework of principles for rationing health care
explicitly, Gormally lists a number of issues, though the list is not
exhaustive:

• What is health? What is health care?
• What is to count as a health-care need (as distinct from wants and
  demands)?
• What positive and negative moral norms should be respected (positive norms might embrace justice, beneficent concern for the individual
  patient, truthfulness; negative norms might embrace not intentionally
  harming patients, not abandoning those in care, not lying)?

Gormally does not pretend that producing, and getting broad agreement
for, a detailed framework for rationing will be easy. Indeed, quite the
reverse is the case since if there is to be explicit rationing then 'a much
more complex framework for rationing decisions than exists at present'
will be necessary.

To undertake this near impossible task, Gormally (1996: 11) favours
a standing Royal Commission which would debate the issues in depth.
Such a body should not be composed of the great and the good since
all too often they are 'so chosen as merely to reflect the paralysing
weaknesses of public policy debates in our society'.

That any legitimate form of explicit rationing would need to meet
these two preconditions might be considered a tall order. The likelihood
of ever achieving Gormally's principled approach to explicit rationing
seems remote indeed. In particular is it conceivable for a Royal Commission to engage seriously with the substantive questions listed above
which, for Gormally, is an essential 'precondition for any worthwhile

Table 2.1 **The players in rationing health care**

	General public %	Doctors %	Managers %
Hospital consultants	61	68	57
GPs	49	68	71
Managers (local health authorities)	25	Question not asked	65
General public	22	30	52
Hospital nurses	19	21	22
Managers (Department of Health/NHS Executive)	16	23	26
Current patients	9	8	9
National politicians	6	18	36
Local politicians	3	6	11
All of the above	3	18	21
Don't know	5	2	—

Source: Heginbotham (1993).

Table 2.2 **Who should set priorities?**

	No. of respondents	Percentage
Doctors	1104	56
Health authorities	377	19
Public	336	17
NHS managers	89	5
Central government and politicians	61	3

Source: Bowling (1996).

consensus that might make approaches to health care rationing more nearly reasonable than they are at present' (1996: 11)? In Chapter 6 we present arguments to show why such an objective, though laudable, is a forlorn hope within the confines of our political system and prevailing approach to the construction of public policy.

Who should set priorities and ration?

There are five main groups of stakeholders who are candidates for this role: the medical profession, health authorities and their managers, the public, government and the courts. Of these, repeated surveys of public opinion show that doctors are accorded highest legitimacy as the group who should make decisions on which treatment should take a higher priority (see Table 2.1). For instance, Bowling (1996) found in her study that while most people interviewed wanted to be involved in the planning of health services, three quarters thought that the responsibility for rationing spending on health care should rest with doctors rather than managers, health authorities or the government (see Table 2.2). The survey also revealed that people thought health authorities should listen to the public's views on health priorities to add legitimacy to their decision-making given their own position as appointed, and not democratically elected, bodies. They also need to be seen by the public to be working with, and not against, their clinical colleagues in priority-setting/rationing exercises. Only in this way could the public's trust be retained. Table 2.1 also reveals that even among doctors themselves and managers, it is doctors who are seen as the most obvious group responsible for deciding priorities when resources are constrained. Although managers have most faith in the public taking such decisions, it is not shared by the public themselves. There is no significant support among the public, doctors or, to a lesser degree, managers for politicians making such decisions.

It is precisely because of the high esteem in which the medical profession is held that rationing by clinical autonomy is able to occur without a public outcry. Much of the debate around the extent to which rationing should be explicit rather than remain implicit arises because of a growing perception that doctors are not best placed to make rationing decisions, especially if the drivers are financial rather than clinical. In addition, many doctors no longer wish to perform this function for reasons returned to later. Examples of doctors withholding treatment on moral grounds, including patients with allegedly aberrant lifestyles (e.g. smokers, drug abusers), have heightened public awareness of the dilemma. General Medical Council rules are unequivocal that patients in need of treatment must not be denied it on moral grounds. To be found guilty of such malpractice would constitute grounds for being struck off the medical register. Nevertheless, the suspicion lingers that ostensibly clinical decisions may not always be strictly clinical. On the other hand, to assert, as many do, that the solution lies in having clear and explicit guidelines to ration treatment is to miss the point which is that clinical decisions may all too easily mask what are in fact decisions based on moral grounds. It is hard to see how explicit guidelines in themselves would be an improvement on the current situation.

Following the NHS changes introduced in 1991 with their emphasis on a purchaser–provider separation, rationing decisions are increasingly falling on health authorities and managers. Although they are expected to consult widely, NHS managers and the non-executive directors of health authorities lack any independent legitimacy as decision-makers, especially at a local level. They are agents of the Secretary of State and are appointed to do their bidding. There is no representation from local interests on health authorities. Managers' own unease at being placed in the position of having to take rationing decisions, with their value-laden and ethical implications, combined with the criticism that the NHS suffers from a 'democratic deficit' as a result of the 'new magistracy' (Stewart 1992) now in charge of significant areas of public policy, including health, has added to calls for central government to give leadership in matters of rationing. Other commentators (Clarke, Hunter and Wistow 1995, 1997; Cooper *et al*. 1995; Coote and Hunter 1996) have suggested, as part of a fresh look at local governance, that local authorities should take over health commissioning thereby subjecting the process of decision-making to democratic control. The principle advocated is that in a democracy a system of elected authorities has to be preferable to a system of appointed bodies. The Association of Metropolitan Authorities (AMA) has also proposed similar reforms given local government's growing influence on health matters (AMA 1993). Pilot schemes are recommended initially to test the idea. The present position whereby unelected and only remotely accountable managers are acting as rationing agents is seen as unsatisfactory and untenable.

Various moves to involve the public in NHS affairs have developed in recent years under the government's *Local Voices* initiative but there is still much experimentation and learning going on (NHS Management Executive 1992). Few models of good practice exist although mechanisms like health panels, focus groups and citizens' juries are regarded as potentially more useful than large-scale public opinion surveys. There also tends to be a concentration on consultation in preference to active involvement by the public at the early stages of policy development. Finally, there is the matter of what happens to the views of the public once (and however) elicited. Are they adhered to, even in part, or quietly ignored? Is feedback forthcoming on how final decisions have been taken and on what grounds? The issue of public involvement is revisited in Chapter 4.

Central government clearly has a degree of legitimacy in health-care rationing since the NHS is accountable through the Secretary of State for Health to Parliament. The Conservative government 1979–97 steered clear of taking a lead on rationing, preferring to leave the responsibility with health authorities and clinicians on the not unreasonable grounds that they are closer to, and therefore more knowledgeable about, local circumstances and situations as well as clinical needs. The problem with a localist approach of this nature is that it allows marked variations to exist between different parts of the UK. Whether this is a problem or not depends on how far a *national* health service is seen to provide a uniform set of services delivered to a common standard or on whether it is perceived as legitimate for local communities to vary the mix according to local preferences. The Conservative government's view was that it was all a matter of balance. A *degree* of local variation can be tolerated, indeed is to be positively welcomed, but it must not be allowed to undermine what remains a national service operating within a national policy framework and adhering to the same common set of principles. Governments in some other countries have sought a different approach in tackling this problem, often by taking a firm national lead. Few, however, have succeeded.

Finally, the courts could become increasingly involved in health policy and resource-allocation decisions (Kennedy 1993). So far, their role has been minimal but a more rights-conscious public, fuelled by the *Patient's Charter*, and a general increase in consumerist behaviour, seems likely to result in resort to the courts for the redress of grievances. The lack of any democratic control over health authorities only exacerbates the problem. So far, the courts have been reluctant to enter into the treacherous waters surrounding rationing as the Child B case amply demonstrated (see Chapter 1, Box 1.1) but this may not always remain the case. In particular, if the government did decide to ration explicitly by determining a list of services and treatments to be included in the NHS, then the courts might see a role for themselves in adjudicating over what services and technologies could be included in the list. At present, however, there is certainly no great enthusiasm for the courts to have a major role in rationing. Nor do they see themselves having one.

Although not a coherent group of stakeholders, there are various experts who would wish to play a more influential role in rationing decisions. Many of these groups, notably public health physicians and health-service researchers (most prominently health economists), have become influential as a result of the development of the NHS R&D strategy (introduced in 1991) and the related rise of the evidence-based medicine (EBM) movement. These initiatives have resulted in the rapid emergence of an evidence-based complex which has provided opportunities to the scientific community to generate data to inform rationing decisions and to influence practice. But EBM, with its biomedical and technocratic bias, risks being accused of encouraging a narrow scientism. It is not regarded as an unmixed blessing as is discussed in Chapter 4.

The options

In meeting the problem of priority-setting or rationing in health care, five broad options may be considered: increased expenditure, greater efficiency, voluntary restraint, explicit rationing, and a policy of (masterly) inactivity. As Boyd (1979) points out, all these options raise difficulties and moral questions which are hard to avoid (conversely, some of them may also be hard to confront). Each is briefly considered in turn in this chapter but are revisited in more detail in Chapter 6 when reviewing future prospects for rationing health care.

Increased expenditure

While possible in theory (and some would say in practice given the public's repeatedly stated wish to pay higher taxes if convinced the additional resources would go to health services), it seems unlikely to be a long-term option. In part this is for reasons so eloquently, if depressingly, articulated by J.K. Galbraith in his thesis on the culture of contentment (Galbraith 1993). The thesis contends that government is perceived as a burden by the 'contented majority' who oppose any social expenditure that is not of direct benefit to them. While the NHS remains the source of health care for the majority of the population this need not remain the case. If the NHS were to become vulnerable to an exodus on the part of the contented classes, it is unlikely that calls for its funding to be increased would be forthcoming any longer. The relationship between public services and taxation is a complex one. Even if health care is seen as an exception it is no guarantee of increased funding especially when the culture of contentment is only concerned with the here and now and not with longer-run consequences. As Galbraith puts it in regard to using taxes to reduce inequality, 'here the collision between wise social action and the culture of contentment is most apparent' (1993: 179) as there is virtually no constituency in favour of tackling inequality through taxation. Furthermore, spending on health must also compete with spending on other services, like education, which are seeking additional investment and are also seen as deserving causes. While modest increases in health spending may be forthcoming they will not be sufficient to meet all the demands on them (Ham 1996). Such pessimism is not universally shared and is considered further in Chapter 6 when looking to the future. For example, Dixon and New (1997) argue that there is no satisfactory answer to the question of whether the NHS is underfunded because the answer requires value judgements, on which opinions will differ.

Greater efficiency

The search for improved efficiency has been a mainstay of central government policy since the first major reorganization of the NHS in 1974. Cost improvements and efficiency gains have been sought annually and have been achieved. A battery of other measures have been launched to secure this objective, ranging from management costs exercises through attempts to tackle clinical inefficiencies to clinical guidelines, evidence-based medicine and related initiatives (although in theory, and in practice, EBM could lead to increased costs). Efforts to root out interventions shown to be ineffective have so far been less successful than attempts to achieve efficiency gains in non-clinical areas. Yet the most significant resources are tied up in clinical activities. Either management has failed to manage the activity for which it is responsible or else the information required to challenge clinical priorities is lacking. The truth probably lies somewhere between these extremes although it is possible to exaggerate the problems over poor or non-existent information and make them an excuse for lack of management action (Burns 1996). We return to this issue in Chapter 3. Meantime, suffice it to say that while achieving greater efficiency has occurred to a marked degree in the NHS and in other health-care systems, inroads into clinical areas have been less successful principally because they have not occurred. Yet the potential for efficiency gains in the clinical sphere is considerable as the proponents of EBM proclaim (Eddy 1994; Timmins 1996).

Voluntary restraint

Trying to dissuade people from seeking assistance from health services on the grounds that they might be better occupied looking to their own lifestyles with a view to modifying them in line with best practice and advice offered by health-promotion specialists and suchlike is not really feasible or politically attractive. Although self-care has developed and a growing minority of people are opposed to the meddlesome nature of much modern medicine, particularly high-tech, heroic surgical interventions, the majority of the public remains stubbornly wedded to health services and in particular to those provided in their local hospital. Attempts to rationalize or reconfigure these invariably unleash vociferous local opposition and accusations of cost-cutting and rationing. Whatever the motivations of managers and the merits of service reconfiguration which can result in mergers or closures, the public's negative response is based on a mixture of emotion, ignorance of the issues (often because they have not been clearly explained) and a deep suspicion, verging on mistrust, of managers who are not seen to have patients' interests to the fore. In such a climate voluntary restraint therefore offers no quick or easy means of reducing pressure on health services.

Rationing

This option is the subject of this book so it will not be exhausted here. Given the problems with, or limitations of, the three options reviewed so far, rationing may seem the only rational option worthy of serious attention. A great variety of rationing systems or devices can be identified and a list of some of these was presented earlier. Some are based on demographic criteria, others on clinical, social or geographic ones; some operate according to an ability to pay, others according to stated and ranked preferences. Common to all of these systems is the view that rationing cannot be avoided. But while there may be a widely shared view about this, *any* rationing system will disadvantage some people and be seen as unfair no matter how explicit it is (indeed, paradoxically, the more explicit it is, the more unfair it might seem). Little wonder, then, that rationing has become a pejorative term which has come to mean denying access to health care principally on the grounds of cost containment (Baker 1995).

Linked to the various systems of rationing is the issue of how it should occur: implicitly or explicitly. In many health-care systems, especially those of a non-market type, rationing has occurred implicitly. Decisions about treating or not treating patients were seen to be taken on clinical grounds and not on grounds of available resources. But market, or quasi-market systems, function in ways which make rationing explicit and it is possible for the public to be made aware of decisions to treat or not treat being taken on grounds other than strictly clinical ones. There are advantages and disadvantages in respect of both implicit and explicit approaches to rationing and these are reviewed in Chapter 6.

Inactivity

A policy of inactivity, masterly or otherwise, is probably the most difficult option to defend publicly, although privately it may be the one most favoured by at least some politicians, managers and professionals (Boyd 1979). It may also be the one which is actually adopted in some form in preference to more active or aggressive policy options such as explicit rationing or increased expenditure. It can also operate reasonably happily alongside other measures such as the continuing search for greater efficiency so long as these do not encroach too heavily on clinical territory since the goodwill and support of clinicians is needed to allow the *status quo* to continue more or less unchallenged.

There is a sixth option which has been termed 'muddling through elegantly' (Hunter 1993a). It seeks to capture the complexities of rationing while at the same time acknowledging the need for improvements in how rationing decisions are made. It also firmly rejects the rampant utilitarianism of rational rationers who want national politicians to give leadership and set clear boundaries to what the NHS will and will not include. Finally, muddling through elegantly is an admission that some choices are so difficult and complex that they probably cannot be made and certainly not with public agreement or consensus. The most (and best) that can be hoped for is improved muddling through. But to argue for its rejection, as rational rationers do, is both naïve and disingenuous. The option, muddling through elegantly, is considered further in Chapter 6. It provides a connecting thread running through the book.

The rhetoric of rationing

Rationing has become a pejorative term conjuring up wartime images of scarcity, deprivation and denial. It is frequently employed not to aid rational debate but, in Baker's words, 'to condemn, to shock, or to scandalise' (Baker 1995: 57). But the adoption of the term on a widespread basis has accompanied the reform of health-care services in many countries over the past decade or so which has been based on market-style concepts and principles. As Loughlin (1996: 149) has pointed out, 'the intellectual character of the rationing debate is shaped and limited by certain assumptions of market economics, the key one being the central economic assumption of "scarcity"'. As far as the UK NHS is concerned, the key difference between the 1991 changes and earlier ones was the attempt explicitly to adopt the language and thinking of markets and private sector management. It is no coincidence that talk of rationing health care began in earnest from this time. Up until then only the odd reference to rationing could be found in the literature.

Far more discussion occurred around the notion of priority-setting – the term that was preferred by the Conservative government. But terms like 'priority-setting', 'choices' and 'planning' have their origins in planned, hierarchical, command-and-control systems rather than devolved market-style ones. Such a planned system characterized the NHS up until the 1991 changes which deliberately sought to overturn them. As Pollock and her colleagues (1995) point out, the internal market is seen as the determinant of who has access to treatment and care. As such, economic factors now play a more substantive role in rationing than notions of health-care needs.

In the US, an interesting discourse has taken place between economists on the meaning of the term rationing in both a US and a European context. Whereas most American economists use the term 'rationing' to mean a non-market allocation of resources whereby those who have the means to pay for care are denied it, European economists conceive of rationing more broadly as denying medically necessary health care or failing to meet medical need. Rationing can therefore be discussed in a context of universal health-care coverage since it is not axiomatically linked to considerations of payment for care by an individual. But this conception of rationing also applies to the US if the view is accepted that rationing is practised by all health-care systems. The issue is not one of *whether* but *how*. In the US, rationing occurs by limiting services according to the ability to pay. Uninsured persons in the US receive fewer resources than insured persons although in the definition of rationing adopted by many American economists the denial of health care to uninsured persons would not be called rationing.

At issue in these differing conceptions of rationality is whether it is irrational or immoral to allocate scarce health-care resources by means of the market with its emphasis on ability to pay rather than according to medical need. In principle, it would be impossible to ration in non-market systems because access is determined by medical need and not ability to pay. Markets therefore ration irrationally and possibly immorally as well if judged by the principles of social justice which hold health care to be deemed a fundamental human right and not a commodity to be bought and sold like any other.

The issue then arises of how medical need is defined and by whom. There are two models: the market conception of consumer or patient demand, and the professional conception of expert-determined health-care need. Klein (1995: 250) usefully contrasts these two models.

If the language of demands is that of the market, the language of needs is that of paternalism. If the market assumes consumer sovereignty, paternalism assumes producer sovereignty ... [A]ccepting the case for paternalism would seem to imply accepting also the case for the private government of public health by those who know best. So it is perhaps not surprising that ... the arena of health care [in Britain] was characterised ... by the dominance of paternalist rationalisers in what was largely a self-contained introspective world.

At issue between the two models is that whereas market conceptions of health care treat it as a commodity much like any other, non-market systems replace consumer sovereignty with health-care experts. Rationing in a market system amounts to a failure to meet patient (i.e. consumer) demand; in a non-market system it amounts to a failure to meet expert-determined need. Compounding the complexities associated with each model are a host of related issues: overuse or underuse of medical resources, the provision of medically unnecessary treatments, the efficacy of medical interventions and evidence (if any) about their outcomes, patients' insistence on receiving futile treatments, trust between doctor and patient, explicit versus implicit rationing (the former being a feature of market systems, the latter a feature of expert-determined ones), and so on.

Chapter 3 goes into greater detail about the adoption of a quasi-market model in the UK NHS from 1991 which resulted in the issue of rationing becoming a matter of growing public concern in keeping with the shift from a paternalistic system of determining health-care needs and allocating resources to a more market-oriented one. The remainder of this chapter describes the essentially paternalistic system which prevailed from the origins of the NHS in 1948 up until 1991: a period of some 43 years. Such a system was also notable for its unitary structure, its emphasis on command and control systems, and its commitment, from the 1970s, to planning and priority-setting in order to ensure that resources were allocated equitably and according to medically determined needs and priorities.

From priority-setting to rationing

For most of its 50-year existence the UK NHS has eschewed market approaches to allocating resources and determining priorities. Centred as these approaches are on the individual, the NHS has pursued an alternative approach: that is, one based on the collective and on meeting its needs. As a result this has accorded considerable power and influence to those providing and (in more recent times) managing health care. They have served as proxies for the patient or consumer and, as a consequence, have been charged with the responsibility for determining whose needs should be met, which needs should be met and how they should be met. In an administered system, in contrast to a managed one, which the NHS was up until the early 1980s and the advent of general management, resources are allocated and needs are met according to bureaucratic systems of planning and priority-setting.

Despite the critics of such mechanisms, who favoured devolved, looser, quasi-market mechanisms of the type introduced in 1991 (although, paradoxically, the NHS is now considerably more centralized than it ever was before the introduction of market-style arrangements), planning and priority-setting did not become established in the

NHS until the mid-1970s. Even then, it is reasonable to argue that such mechanisms did not so much fail, as their critics allege, as that they were never given a chance to succeed because of constant political interference and tinkering with the structure of the NHS (Barnard 1991) – a charge that has also been levelled at the post-1991 changes which their proponents maintain have never been given a chance to prove themselves. The real problem was a loss of faith and credibility in the public sector, and its ability to deliver, to be replaced by unbridled enthusiasm for largely untested ideas such as competition and privatization within the public sector. The root causes may go even deeper and certainly wider than the UK or health policy in isolation. Commenting on the state of health policy in America, Thompson (1981: 1) asserts:

If the 1960s featured confidence that government could successfully attack inequities, the 1970s witnessed a shattering of this confidence. Complaints about under-performance, delay, and soaring costs abound. Doubt that government can make things work dominates the thinking of much of the public as well as many government decision makers and academic students of public policy.

Little wonder then that markets rather than hierarchies appeared so attractive to politicians of all persuasions disillusioned by the rigidities and lacklustre performance of the public sector with its sterile corporate planning systems.

As Mooney *et al.* (1992) note, given the endless debate in the NHS about priorities and how to set them it is surprising that it took until 1976 for the first document on priority-setting to appear (Department of Health and Social Security (DHSS) 1976) – more than a quarter of a century after the formation of the NHS. Clearly, priorities had been set prior to this time but they did not embrace health services as a whole. The priorities document's antecedents lay in the 1962 Hospital Plan which was the first formal attempt to plan hospital services on a rational basis but it was the priorities document which took a comprehensive look at the NHS as a whole and stated publicly which services and client (or care) groups should be accorded priority. It was also a consultative document. After 1974, the NHS became responsible for *health*, and not merely *hospital* care. Indeed, the attempt to loosen the hospital service's domination of the NHS and its consumption of around 70 per cent of total expenditure was the key motivation for establishing a planning framework. Planning was seen as vital to the success of the 1974 NHS reorganization with its aim of allocating resources on a more rational, coherent basis and shifting the balance of care away from an exclusive focus on hospitals.

As the 1976 consultative document on priorities for the health and personal social services candidly acknowledged, it marked 'the first time an attempt has been made to establish rational and systematic priorities throughout the health and personal social services' (DHSS 1976: 1). The document set differentially higher growth rates for personal social services as against health services and for the priority groups compared with acute and maternity services. These priorities were broadly accepted in the NHS although there was concern over whether the desired switch in resources could be achieved. The priorities guidance which finally emerged in 1977 (DHSS 1977) was toned down from firm targets to hopeful aspirations reflecting the realities of central–local relations in the NHS. The reservations expressed by health authorities at the consultative stage were sufficiently persuasive to lead central government to adopt a less directive and more *laissez-faire* approach.

Subsequent guidance on priorities (e.g. DHSS 1981) was similarly non-prescriptive. Indeed, it went further in this direction, abandoning any attempt to express priorities in terms of targets for service levels or financial allocations. No benchmarks existed against which to measure progress towards national priorities. This reflected a new mood in government. A philosophy of *laissez-faire* had taken a firm hold of the NHS by the late 1970s in response to growing disillusionment with the centralist, managerial philosophy which had pervaded the service since 1974. There was a loss of faith in planning and in direct intervention by the centre in local affairs. In its consultative document, *Patients First*, announcing the shift in approach, the Conservative government promised 'the minimum of interference by any central authority' in the affairs of local health authorities and a 'simpler planning system' freed from 'over-complicated and bureaucratic' arrangements (DHSS and Welsh Office 1979). The approach to priority-setting fell victim to these new arrangements. However, they proved short-lived. The new philosophy of devolution created a vacuum in the chain of accountability whereby if the Secretary of State was intent on divesting him or herself of numerous responsibilities how could (s)he be held to account to Parliament for all that happened in the NHS?

Almost from the outset, then, the *laissez-faire* philosophy was destined for revision. Powerful criticisms of the policy came from two parliamentary committees: the influential Public Accounts Committee (House of Commons Public Accounts Committee 1981) and the Social Services Committee (House of Commons Social Services Committee 1980). They maintained that there were strict limits on how far the DHSS could go in detaching itself from the periphery's use of resources and setting of priorities. The Conservative government's response to these criticisms was to tighten its grip on the NHS. With the introduction of general management in the early 1980s, and the appearance of the national health strategy in 1992 (Secretary of State for Health 1992), there was a gradual tightening of the centre's position and renewed efforts made to shift priorities within the NHS. In fact, the 1992 health strategy was the first attempt by any government to produce a strategy for health as distinct from an exclusive focus on health-care services. The *Health of the Nation* (Secretary of State for Health 1992) was derived from WHO Health for All principles and heralded a return to a planning approach which in some respects resembled the earlier attempts in the mid-1970s. It is fair to conclude, therefore, that the oscillation in centre–local relations has been a constant feature of the NHS since its inception as both national and local stakeholders search for the optimal balance between the extremes of centralization on the one hand and local delegation on the other (Hunter 1983).

Conclusion

Through the late 1970s and the whole of the 1980s, the word 'priorities' was more commonly used than the 'R' word: 'rationing'. At macro and meso levels, priority-setting and planning were the principal mechanisms employed over this period to allocate resources to care sectors and client groups. At a micro level, the notion of clinical autonomy served a similar purpose for the individual patient and the meeting of their needs. It created the illusion that decisions about whether or not to treat a condition and how were the result of clinical considerations rather than resource constraints.

Aaron and Schwartz (1984), whose comparative work on rationing was cited earlier, maintain that British clinicians have colluded in this arrangement as the price they must pay for retaining their freedoms, status and privileges. They suggest that 'physicians are asserting that the treatment is *medically* optimal or very close to optimal, that patients denied care or provided with alternative forms of care because of budget limits lose essentially nothing of medical significance' (Aaron and Schwartz 1984: 101). They go on:

> The British physician often seems to adjust his [*sic*] indications for treatment to bring into balance the demand for care and the resources available to provide it. This kind of rationalisation preserves as much as possible the feeling that all care of value is being provided ... Most patients in Britain appear willing to accept their doctor's word if he says that no further treatment of a particular disease is warranted.
>
> (p. 111)

Whether this acquiescence or passivity on the part of patients is the result of a lack of knowledge about possible treatments or of an abiding trust in the doctor's word or of the deference to be found in paternalistic systems of provision, or of something else altogether is unclear. It needs further exploration.

In contrast to what the majority of patients think, not all doctors believe they are providing potentially beneficial or adequate care to their patients. Many have come to believe that they are acting as society's (unwilling) agents or accomplices in rationing care. While most were content, at least up until the 1991 NHS changes, to find medical rationales for what was fiscally necessary, over the past few years there have been growing calls for doctors to be relieved of the responsibility for taking what are in effect rationing decisions and for central government to state clearly and openly what the NHS is to cover and not cover by way of treatments.

The reasons for this shift are described and assessed in Chapter 3 but they have their origins, in large measure, in the attempt to reduce clinical freedom by managing clinical work and holding doctors to account for what they do. These encroachments on doctors' freedom, combined with intensifying financial pressures, resulted in many doctors at the time of the 1991 reforms acknowledging that the concordat between the profession and the State, whereby the State granted freedoms and privileges to allow the profession to practise medicine in the way it preferred and wished in return for doctors making decisions on clinical grounds about the treatment of individual patients, was rapidly being undermined as the 'cult of managerialism', the language of markets and the rise of consumerism swept through the NHS. Doctors were not immune from these developments and could hardly be expected to be. The upshot was that life (and death) would never be the same again. Rationing was firmly on the agenda.

The Health-Care Rationing Debate in the UK: a Review

PART TWO

The Health-Care Rationing Debate
in the UK: a Review

CHAPTER 3

The management agenda

Introduction

This chapter and the next are concerned with how the issue of rationing health care has manifested itself and been tackled in the UK from the early 1990s to the present. This chapter explores the reasons for health-care rationing becoming a major public policy problem in the early 1990s. Particular consideration is given to the impact of the NHS internal market and competitive mechanisms, introduced in 1991, since these have been instrumental in contributing to the 'loss of innocence' whereby explicit rationing has emerged as a key issue (Harrison and Hunter 1994). Although, as we saw in the last chapter, resources have never been sufficiently plentiful to do all that may be possible, the assumption had prevailed that any limits to what was prescribed by way of medical care were a result of medical need and not budget limits. The adoption of market-style mechanisms shattered this illusion and forced both the public and health-care practitioners to acknowledge, if they had been left in any doubt, that finance *was* a major factor in determining how health-care resources were distributed. Coupled with a focus on empowering users to be more involved and assertive in expressing their preferences, even if it had more the appearance of gesture politics than a serious attempt to shift the balance of power in favour of users, it was virtually certain that rationing would become a hotly contested issue. And so it has proved.

Assessing the impact of the 1991 NHS changes in any objective sense poses something of a difficulty because of the limited nature of much of the published evidence available (Robinson and Le Grand 1994). This chapter therefore relies on what limited completed published research and other sources exist, including those to which the author has contributed, as well as material which, though in the public domain, is not widely accessible. Use, though non-attributable, is also made of other intelligence acquired through the author's close involvement in the NHS business, in particular as a non-executive director of a large metropolitan health authority, and as an observer and analyst over many years of the evolution of health-policy and health-systems reforms both in the UK and overseas.

The 1991 NHS changes

The proposals for NHS reform which appeared in the 1989 White Paper, *Working for Patients*, and subsequently enshrined in the 1990 NHS and Community Care Act and implemented in 1991, did not emerge from nowhere. Much of the groundwork for them had been laid almost a decade earlier with the introduction of general management following the recommendations of the NHS Management Inquiry Team led by Roy Griffiths who subsequently become the Conservative government's health adviser and had a significant input into the events and deliberations culminating in the 1989 White Paper.

The significance of Griffiths

To understand the significance of the Griffiths management changes, it is necessary to say something about the state of NHS management prior to their introduction. A very brief account is presented here; other sources provide more extensive description and analysis (Harrison 1988; Harrison *et al.* 1992; Klein 1996).

Although there was much talk of management in the NHS prior to the Griffiths report, especially in the run-up to the first major NHS reorganization in 1974, it in no way threatened, or sought to destabilize or seriously disturb, the prevailing power balance. The government and medical profession continued to enjoy what amounted to a cosy corporatist relationship in which doctors, or rather their representatives, had direct access to ministers. Part of this corporatist ethos resulted in the design of formal organizational arrangements in such a way as to leave doctors largely free from day-to-day management, and to leave members of other clinical professions managed only by other members of their own profession. Despite early calls in the 1960s for the creation of non-medically qualified chief executive posts (Joint Working Party 1967; Hunter 1984; Scottish Health Services Council 1996), the NHS continued to be administered by groups of managers from a mix of professional backgrounds. Indeed, the 1974 management arrangements involved the creation of multidisciplinary management teams of chief officers taking decisions only by consensus: that is, where no member disagreed and each had a right of veto. Despite their involvement in the team decision-making process, doctors remained largely outside the subject matter of that process.

But at least as important in preserving doctors' freedom from management was the doctrine of 'clinical freedom': the notion that a fully-qualified doctor cannot be directed in their clinical work. This notion underpinned the creation of the NHS, its first reorganization in 1974 and all subsequent changes up until the Griffiths report in 1983. Interestingly, this was a period when the talk was of priority-setting rather than rationing and when doctors appeared reasonably accepting of their role as resource rationers/allocators which they performed by reference to clinical criteria ostensibly governed by, or justified/legitimized according to, need rather than financial restrictions.

There was certainly no intention on the part of government during this period to challenge or undermine doctors' freedom from management control. Indeed, quite the contrary. In the government's White Paper setting out its plans for the 1974 reorganization (DHSS 1972: vii), it was stated clearly that 'The organisational changes will not affect the professional relationship between individual patients and individual professional workers on which the complex of health services is so largely built.'

Clinical freedom, it was acknowledged, 'is cherished by the professions and accepted by the Government'. The philosophy remained intact right up until Griffiths. At the time of the 1982 reorganization the government's earlier consultative document, *Patients First*, had the following to say: 'It is doctors, dentists and nurses and their colleagues in the other health professions who provide the care and cure of patients and promote the health of the people. It is the purpose of management to support them in giving that service' (DHSS and Welsh Office 1979: 1–2).

Despite references elsewhere to the need for efficiency, there is no implication that *doctors* might need to become more efficient; the inference is rather that it is other, unspecified, groups which need to be controlled in order to maximize resources for medical care. Mention is made of the need to establish priorities as resources are tight but there is no direct challenge, or even a whisper of one, to medical autonomy.

Prior to the Griffiths report, therefore, there was no apparent desire for increased managerial control over doctors or for more general management control over other clinical professions. Indeed, such a development was regarded as almost unthinkable and certainly unrealistic. Management was perceived as diplomacy in which every effort was made to reach an accommodation between interested parties in matters of a sensitive or controversial nature (Harrison 1988).

In the pre-Griffiths era, therefore, the conclusion to be drawn from studies of it is that doctors were, and continued to be, the most powerful group in the NHS. Once doctors are disregarded, and trailing some way behind, managers were seen as the most influential among the remaining actors. But any attempt to shift NHS management away from the diplomat role would represent a challenge to medical power, and its success would be crucially dependent on the effectiveness of such a challenge. While occasional breaches of an overall acceptance of medical supremacy or dominance did occur from time to time (see Harrison *et al.* 1992 for some examples), the medical profession's special powers have remained largely and impressively intact. This seemed to exist (and still does) in the ability of doctors to deal with what would otherwise be major uncertainties for managers. Above all, they have (and were willingly accorded) the ability to ration health care in an acceptable manner by calling it something else. Moreover, as was noted in the last chapter, the term itself was rarely used. Rather, managers were in the business of deciding priorities and, within these, doctors decided on the basis of clinical need who received treatment.

As politicians and managers were quick to grasp, no one has much to gain by being seen to deny care. One (ingenious) way of avoiding being thus seen is to leave it to doctors, who not only have the benefit of public legitimacy but can, under the rubric of clinical freedom, make rationing decisions largely invisible. The effect of the Griffiths changes, and the subsequent market-style changes introduced in 1991, was to expose this approach to rationing health care and to challenge its rationality, acceptability and ethical basis. Once the genie was out of the bottle, as it were, and the impact of general management began to be felt, there was no putting it back again. The taboo 'R' word was firmly on the agenda.

Griffiths and general management

By one of those critical but unforeseen quirks of history, the management inquiry team which eventually emerged in the early 1980s was not quite what had been originally envisaged or intended by the then Secretary of State for Social Services, Norman Fowler. What was in fact announced by the Secretary of State was a manpower inquiry in the light of growing unrest among the unions and the industrial action to which the NHS was being subjected.

Roy Griffiths, Deputy Chairman and Managing Director of J. Sainsbury and largely credited with the company's success, was approached to chair the inquiry. But he was reluctant to accept the terms of reference on the grounds that they were overly restrictive and were focused on a second-order problem (Harrison and Wistow 1997). To confine any inquiry to it would, in his opinion, avoid attending to the first-order problem which centred on management. Griffiths only agreed to lead the inquiry team if its terms of reference were widened to include management. Ministers agreed to this and the inquiry's terms of reference were fixed. The inquiry was set two main tasks:

- to examine the ways in which resources are used and controlled inside the health service, so as to secure the best value for money and the best possible services for the patient
- to identify what further management issues need pursuing for these important purposes.

The emphasis of the inquiry team was to be on 'management action' which meant a quick, clearly focused review of the problem with recommendations for action – all to be covered in a succinct statement rather than a lengthy report in the style of a Royal Commission.

The inquiry team was concerned at the lack of individual management accountability in the NHS and, by implication, was highly critical of the system of consensus management. The chief drawback was that the buck did not stop with any one person but got passed round members of a consensus-management team which, it was claimed, could lead to 'lowest common denominator decisions' and to long delays in the management process. It was difficult to know who was in charge. In a famous sentence, Griffiths wrote: 'If Florence Nightingale were carrying her lamp through the corridors of the NHS today, she would almost certainly be searching for the people in charge' (NHS Management Inquiry 1983: 22). Generally, in the team's opinion, management in the NHS lacked drive and thrust. It was too concerned with policy maintenance rather than change, and seemed to emphasize and endorse a producer orientation in preference to a consumer one. The solution to this state of managerial malaise, the team believed, was to introduce a system of general management which would focus management effort and clarify where responsibility lay and with whom. It would also counter the criticism that the NHS suffered from over-administration and under-management.

The medical profession was seen as central in the drive to strengthen management. Indeed, to howls of anguish from nurses, Griffiths referred to doctors as the 'natural managers'. He wanted them fully involved in, and committed to, the management task. Clinical doctors were to become actively involved in management by being responsible for management budgets.

Whether the Griffiths proposals amounted to a management revolution may be overstating its impact. Certainly, a great deal of 'hype', much of it manufactured by the government, accompanied its appearance and subsequent rapid implementation. There was also certainly a Messianic, crusading dimension well captured by Strong and Robinson (1990: 3) in their study of general management.

[T]his was not just another way of structuring the health service, it was also a crusade ... general management ... was an efficiency drive ... but ... it was also, or so it was hoped, a far better way of running health services; a way in which higher quality care would be delivered from coordinated frontline workers. Down the tatty corridors of the NHS, new and dedicated heroes would stride – the general managers. Inspired by their leadership a new sort of staff would arise. Armed with better information and new techniques from the private sector, much more closely monitored yet working as a team, they would at last take collective pride in their work – and responsibility for it.

Griffiths heralded the break with the diplomat style of management which had prevailed hitherto. This occurred through the creation of general manager posts and the concomitant loss of professional influence generally and specifically of the medical veto on the former consensus-management teams. Doctors were quick to express concern at what they saw as possible encroachment on their territory by a lay manager instructing them on what to do regardless of whether or not it was in patients' best interests. The shift in management style was acutely pinpointed by Day and Klein (1983: 1813). It was a 'move from a system that is based on the mobilisation of consent to one based on the management of conflict – from one that has conceded the right of groups to veto change to one that gives the managers the right to override objections'. General management, as Harrison *et al.* (1992: 49–50) put it, can therefore be seen 'as, in principle, the antithesis of the 1974 system of consensus team decision-making; just as this was a device for both maintaining professional autonomy of doctors and for maintaining the career aspirations of the other clinical professions, so the advent of general management threatened both'.

The subsequent NHS changes, announced in the 1989 White Paper, *Working for Patients*, took further the cult of managerialism which Griffiths had started some years before and further shifted the frontier between medicine and management firmly in favour of management One consequence of this progressive shift during the second half of the 1980s and early 1990s was an end to the unstated concordat between the government and the medical profession that in return for a significant measure of clinical autonomy doctors would in effect, and to put it bluntly, ration health care, albeit cloaked in terms of clinical judgement as to the most appropriate course of action.

From hierarchies to markets

In many respects the government's proposals for further organizational and management changes, announced in the 1989 White Paper, *Working for Patients*, and produced in response to growing concern about the possible underfunding of the NHS, were a rather confused, conflicting *mélange* of theories and rationales. The source of the problem – alleged underfunding – was ignored completely. Instead, the government sought to improve supply-side efficiency and effectiveness by introducing market-style incentives and by further strengthening management following the Griffiths changes, introduced in 1984, which were just beginning to bed down. The 1989 proposals were presented as a natural extension of the management-strengthening started by Griffiths, only this time the government's obvious enthusiasm for private sector management practices was thinly veiled.

But certain features of the changes represented an odd and uneasy mix of the old (hierarchies, command-and-control systems) and the new (markets and competition) which did not really sit well together – as, indeed, subsequently proved to be the case. For instance, much was made in the 1989 White Paper of the chain of management command which, as a result of the introduction of general management, ran from districts through regions to the NHS Chief Executive and through him to the Secretary of State and then Parliament. But, as Harrison *et al.* (1992: 119) point out:

this was rather a curious cuckoo in the nest of the provider market. Markets, of any kind, are not run by a single clear chain of command. On the contrary 'a market system is a "spontaneous order" monitored by its feedbacks, it conflicts with a "rational order" shaped by targets' (Sartori 1987: 400).

In fact, and somewhat ironically in the circumstances, the command-and-control notion for all the stress placed on it did not really fit the pre-1984 NHS since a chain of command did not exist. Paradoxically, in view of his wish to decentralize responsibility, putting such a chain of command in place was Griffiths' legacy to the NHS, although whether he appreciated how politicized it would allow NHS management to become is unclear, but probably doubtful. He simply saw that what worked in business might usefully be transferred and tried in a public service and may not have appreciated how difficult it would be to separate politics from policy in a service that was becoming more politicized as resources became ever tighter and as media interest in health issues grew. A chain of command is clearly attractive to ministers who were probably always ambivalent about letting go were a market style approach to develop and take off. It allowed them to intervene at will with a machine ready to respond to their commands and it provided a means of claiming that public accountability was effective. Curiously, this ambivalence about encouraging markets on the one hand while being reluctant to let central control go on the other has resulted in an even tighter central grip on the service than anything which preceded it. It may be a peculiarly British phenomenon. As Hoggett (1996: 27) describes these developments more generally in the restructuring of the public sector in Britain, elements of decentralized, hands-off market-based approaches to delivering public services have been 'dwarfed by visible elements of centralisation . . . and the extended use of hands-on systems of performance management creating a form of "evaluative state"'. For Hoggett, the public sector in Britain in the 1990s exemplifies an 'uneasy combination of the new and the old, the hands-off and the hands-on, the sophisticated and the crude, freedom and surveillance, quality and quantity' (Hoggett 1996: 28). In Handy's (1994: 17–18) words, we should not be dismayed by 'the contradictions and surprises of paradox. [It] has to be *accepted*, coped with and made sense of.'

The excessive degree of centralization and formalization had unforeseen consequences on the dynamics of the NHS. As Jenkins (1995: 88) observed, 'The centralisation of the Service left an uneasy feeling that a professional relationship of trust between patient and doctor and hospital and community had been broken.' Jenkins contrasted the monster created principally by Margaret Thatcher and Kenneth Clarke with Bevan's original model for the NHS: 'His health service was concerned simply with offering doctors and nurses an administrative apparatus "for them freely to use in accordance with their training for the benefit of the people of the country"' (Jenkins 1995: 86). This, in effect, was the profession-led NHS which survived until the Griffiths management changes in the first half of the 1980s. Griffiths questioned this approach and sought to strengthen management in order to shift the emphasis,

Box 3.1 Elements of the new public management

- Hands-on professional management in the public sector.

- Standard-setting, performance measurement, and target-setting, particularly where professionals are involved.

- Emphasis on output controls linked to resource allocation.

- The disaggregation or 'unbundling' of previously monolithic units into purchaser–provider functions, and the introduction of contracting.

- The shift to competition as the key to cutting costs and raising standards.

- Emphasis on private sector management style and a move away from the public service ethic.

- Discipline and parsimony in resource use: cost-cutting, doing more with less.

Source: Adapted from Hood (1991).

and eventually, the balance of power from producers to consumers in line with commercial practice – the world with which he was most familiar. The market rhetoric of the 1989 proposals endorsed this approach and sought to take it further by talk of 'money following the patient', and through GP fundholding which would allow GPs to hold budgets and be able to respond more flexibly and appropriately to patients' wishes.

But the government was never prepared to see the NHS in pure market terms. Rather, the terms 'managed market' and 'managed competition' were employed to make a distinction between the theory of pure markets on the one hand and the government's commitment to a public service, which the NHS remained, on the other. As a former Secretary of State for Health, Virginia Bottomley, told the House of Commons in 1991 at the time the reforms were being implemented, the NHS 'is not a market where the outcome is allowed to fall where it will, because it is a managed public service'. Much of the thinking underpinning the 1991 NHS changes was informed by notions and concepts which have come to be referred to as 'new public management' (Hood 1991). The principal dimensions of new public management (NPM) are listed in Box 3.1.

The NPM was not confined to the NHS or even the UK. It can best be described as an international movement which overtook public administration globally across a range of public policy spheres. Of particular importance was the emphasis in NPM on standard-setting, performance management, and target-setting in the sphere of professional influence. Also important was the emphasis on private sector management and the move away from the traditional public service ethic which owed more to sound administration than management.

In the NHS, the application of NPM principles resulted, *inter alia*, in the introduction of an internal market (Hunter 1993b). This took the form of a purchaser–provider separation of responsibilities and the emergence of a 'contract culture'. The former unified, integrated NHS was disaggregated or 'unbundled' into purchasers (health authorities and GP fundholders) and providers (hospital and community health trusts, and GPs). Business between these groups is transacted through a system of annual contracts, usually of a block type but increasingly of a cost-and-volume type and, more rarely, on a case-by-case basis. Health authorities are also required to produce five-year strategies and trusts are required to produce business plans. These respective documents do not always correspond with, or complement, each other or share the same priorities. Health authorities are required to assess the health needs of their communities and meet these in the most cost-effective way. Provider units bid for contracts to provide services. They are essentially small businesses which have two aims: to maximize income, and expand their services in order to survive.

The upshot of all these developments on the medical profession has been a closer bureaucratic control of its activities. Whether its former dominance is now subject to erosion through deprofessionalization or proletarianization is unclear (Larkin 1993). However, its autonomy is certainly under threat from management as well as from health services researchers intent on challenging medical practice variations and from active consumers.

There is another dimension to be considered when assessing the impact of markets on existing relationships and this concerns the notion of trust. This affects relations between, for instance, doctors and managers and between doctors and patients. The marketization of health care had eroded 'high-trust' relationships (Harrison and Lachmann 1996). Trust implies mutual understanding and respect. Whatever its shortcomings, the pre-1984 NHS was based on 'high-trust' relationships in which the parties involved observed mutual obligations which were not precisely defined. The post-1984 and 1991 changes introduced relationships which imply low trust: everything must be defined, documented, formalized and transformed into a quasi-contractual relationship. In his seminal study of labour-management issues Fox (1974) defined 'high-trust' relationships as ones in which the participants:

- share (or have similar) ends and values
- have a diffuse sense of long-term obligation
- offer support without calculating the cost or expecting an immediate return
- communicate freely and openly with one another
- are prepared to trust the other and risk their own fortunes in the other party

- give the benefit of the doubt in relation to motives and goodwill if there are problems.

'Low-trust' relationships, in contrast, are ones in which the participants:

- have divergent goals and interests
- have explicit expectations which must be reciprocated through balanced exchanges
- carefully calculate the costs and benefits of any concession made
- restrict and screen communications in their own separate interests
- attempt to minimize their dependence on the other's discretion
- are suspicious about mistakes or failures, attributing them to ill will or default and invoke sanctions.

Fox argued that purely economic exchanges and those relying on formal contracts institutionalized the dynamics of low trust and low discretion. Social exchange, conversely, entails judgement in task performance and loyalty and sustains high-trust relationships and high levels of work discretion. Fox claimed that with markets and contractual relations permeating every sector of social and public life, the reciprocity and diffuse obligations essential for high-trust relationships were being progressively undermined. As Flynn, Williams and Pickard (1996: 143) show in their study of contracting in community health services, high-discretion work (e.g. complex professional services) necessitates high levels of trust.

Dogmatic attempts to codify, formalise and prescribe such high-discretion work will not only be unfeasible but also counterproductive, because prescriptive contracts are inappropriate for tasks characterised by indeterminacy and uncertainty, and the use of sanctions (resting upon distrust) will undermine the contractual relationship.

There is much in the description and analysis of trust, and in the shift from high-trust to low-trust relationships in the NHS, which has a direct bearing on the issue of rationing. In high-trust relationships for rationing to remain implicit was not considered to be a problem. Indeed, it was a sign of the strength of the relationship between doctor and manager (where the manager trusted the doctor to operate efficiently and effectively) and between doctor and patient (where the patient trusted the doctor to do all they could to alleviate the presenting problem). But the arrival of markets and aggressive consumerism are eroding high-trust relationships with the result that, along with emerging low-trust relationships, there is an emphasis on explicit rationing and on codifying or defining precisely, clearly and openly what the NHS will and will not cover – which is the equivalent of the contracting process governing transactions between purchasers and providers. Managers are now expected, even if their follow-through is weak, to challenge doctors who may not be practising cost-effectively in their terms, and patients are becoming distrustful of doctors whom they suspect are making decisions not on clinical grounds but on narrow cost-saving ones.

What is important for the present discussion of how health-care rationing appeared high on the policy agenda in the 1990s is not the detail of the 1991 changes or their subsequent evolution and modification, rather it is the cult, or celebration, of managerialism (and notably the particular brand of managerialism known as NPM with its market ethos prominent) and its impact on the medical profession which is of primary interest. This is because of the link which can be traced to the increasing subjugation of doctors to the edicts of the new managerialism, with their emphasis on control and accountability, and doctors' growing reluctance to continue doing the State's bidding as, in effect, 'closet rationers'. The purchaser–provider separation, the cornerstone of the 1991 changes, also had the effect of making explicit and transparent processes which had hitherto remained largely hidden from view and public scrutiny. The need to negotiate contracts with finite sums of money served to make it quite clear what could and could not be purchased with the resources available. Whereas such decisions had previously been taken by individual clinicians who then expected their hospitals and health authorities to pay up, under the post-1991 arrangements hospitals and other facilities do not receive funds except through contracts which specify, more or less precisely, the work to be done, the amount and, possibly, to what quality standard. The key decision-making level is now above that of the individual clinician. Indeed, a major criticism of the 'contract culture' is that doctors have been largely bypassed and excluded from the negotiations between providers and purchasers. The negotiations have been conducted by managers, including directors of public health and medical directors. But frontline consultants can (and do) feel somewhat disenfranchized in the process. This is ironic because a key objective of the changes was to devolve responsibility to the level closest to the patient. Such a shift may have occurred in respect of GP fundholders but not elsewhere. The upshot of all this has been to fuel further doctors' anxiety and hostility to the NHS changes and their growing sense of being taken over by a system and style of management of which they are deeply suspicious.

The concerns of the medical profession are understandable and not entirely without foundation. As Pollitt (1993) argues, the new orthodoxy of managerialism amounted to 'a set of beliefs and practices, at the core of which burns the seldom-tested assumption that better management will prove an effective solvent for a wide range of economic and social ills'. Not only the medical profession but also the public and various commentators and analysts think that the government's management changes are the outcome of a mixture of ideology, pragmatism and fashion rather than based on any empirical assessment of what would and would not work (Coote and Hunter 1996). Even Griffiths, who produced the original report on general management in 1983, which informed the 1989 proposals, and who remained to advise five successive

Secretaries of State, found that even the simplest management concepts became 'saturated with political overtones' (Griffiths 1992: 61–70). He also made it clear that what he had sought to introduce were effective management processes into the NHS and not another parallel profession: general managers. In his opinion, the implementation priorities left much to be desired. As he put it some years later, 'Major policy issues were left uncovered. There was no attempt to establish objectives at the centre, and no concentration on outcomes' (Griffiths 1992).

Griffiths found the government's review of the NHS which resulted in the 1989 White Paper, *Working for Patients*, 'astonishing' (May 1993). Just as general management was finding its feet, it was confronted with new challenges that would have made strenuous demands on well-established management let alone the fledgling process in the NHS. Griffiths also regretted the use of market language since he foresaw that it could only appear confrontational both inside the NHS among professional groups and outside in the public at large. Even if the ideas emanating from right-wing ideologues had been rejected in the proposed changes, the language was not. And, as was noted in the last chapter in relation to the use of language and rationing, language is important even if what it describes is not what actually results or is to be expected. It can sway opinions and people's perceptions and fuel suspicions about what the true intentions of reformers may be. It is certainly likely to lead, as it did in the NHS, to an erosion, and ultimately a breakdown, of trust between those who make policy and those charged with implementing it and making it work. This is what happened between managers and doctors. Managers were increasingly seen as the agents of ministers – mere functionaries in a chain of command put in place by Griffiths' general management changes – rather than as a group of enablers and facilitators who existed primarily to support doctors and make their lives tolerable.

Ironically, in view of their opposition to the concept of an NHS in the first place, doctors saw themselves as the sole remaining guardians of the founding principles of the NHS. As the power balance between doctors and managers shifted seemingly inevitably and inexorably in favour of managers, doctors became increasingly vociferous and strident in their condemnation of the NHS changes in general and the cult of managerialism in particular. Even if, as Gray and Jenkins (1995) conclude, the changes may have been more about form than substance, undoubted signs of major substantive change do exist. The nature of power and politics in the health service has been altered which 'has been at the expense of the professionals and to the advantage of the managers' (Gray and Jenkins 1995: 29). In the interaction between patients, purchasers, politicians and professionals, it is the position of managers which is now pivotal. And it is this development which has contributed significantly to a medical profession which, notwithstanding some exceptions, is increasingly ill at ease with the NHS and the business-oriented trajectory it appears to be on.

Management and the medical profession

Developing the final point of the preceding section, the issue for con-sideration here is the extent to which the changes which flowed from *Working for Patients* have substantively affected medical power at both macro and micro levels. A distinction is to be made between doctor power at macro and micro levels respectively in any assessment of how the 1991 NHS changes have impacted on the medical profes-sion's fairly well-established power base. It is likely to have impacted differentially on each of these levels (Harrison *et al.* 1992). Doctors do appear to have lost out at the macro level as a result of the collapse of the postwar corporatist State. Having been highly influential at this level of high policy during the 1960s and 1970s, they are now just one of many professional associations lobbying government, although having been left out in the cold throughout most of the 1980s and early 1990s the reception they received following Virginia Bottomley's replacement as Secretary of State for Health under the Conservative Government was somewhat warmer.

Arguably, it is at the micro level where doctors have proved them-selves most powerful and resistant to change. As Harrison *et al.* (1992: 140) describe it:

medical micro-power is essentially conservative – it is a power to resist change that comes from outside, to resist not necessarily by battles at meetings and other 'first face' campaigns (though they may also occur) but rather by silent, individualistic non-compliance – a 'second face' refusal to become engaged or involved. That is one reason why it is so hard to beat – medical micro-power is not organised influence.

Whatever else they may have achieved, the 1991 changes further en-hanced the prominence of management and of those performing these roles. Managers lead the contracting process according to which ser-vices will be provided. As part of this, medical work has to be defined and costed more precisely than ever before. The fact that progress on this front may be far slower and less impressive than anticipated does not negate the logic and purpose of the changes to bring about exactly such an outcome.

The new managerialism, in accordance with NPM principles (see Box 3.1), is undermining medical dominance in other ways. In areas of quality and clinical audit, and more recently through the research and development strategy and related notions of clinical effectiveness and evidence-based medicine (EBM), the medical profession is being subjected to more systematic and rigorous managerial assessment and, in the jargon, performance management. Even if quality and audit are presented as educational devices which doctors will operate and apply themselves in the form (and safety) of self-review and peer-review, the reality is that the boundary between medicine and management is being progressively breached. Developments in, *inter alia*, quality, audit and monitoring together constitute 'a significant incursion into the medical domain. They represent a trimming of doctors' micro-power, because they open a management window . . . onto those core medical activities of diagnosis, admissions, prescribing therapies and deciding on discharges' (Harrison *et al.* 1992: 143).

But there are also countervailing pressures which serve to arrest or constrain the advance of management and its assault on clinical autonomy and many of these centre on the rationing dilemma, especially as it operates at a micro level (Hunter 1992; Harrison and Pollitt 1994). After all, doctors' specialist knowledge remains irreplaceable which itself places limits on managers' incursions into medical territory. Also, as has been pointed out in Chapter 2 in the discussion of who should ration health care, there are few eager candidates (and certainly not managers) for the heavy responsibilities and painful uncertainties unavoidably involved in day-to-day clinical decision-making or the rationing which accompanies it. Managers and politicians, on their own admission, remain heavily dependent on the medical profession in these important respects. Paradoxically, however, the effect of the changes on doctors' diminishing autonomy has been to make them reluctant to remain sole arbiters in such decisions at a time when they are not only subject to more managerial meddling and interference but when the public is being encouraged to be more assertive and more consumer-oriented in its demands. Instead of being respected professionals who have been granted important freedoms and discretionary powers, doctors feel dumped on and the 'fall-guys' (and gals) required to enact the government's dirty business. Hence their preference for the term 'rationing' to describe what they see to be happening and for the process to be given a national lead by central government. Rationing's pejorative overtones as an activity are precisely those they wish to emphasize and play up as well as distance themselves from. It is no coincidence that at a time when their professionalism and autonomy are being subjected to greater managerial control, doctors no longer wish or feel able to be responsible for the difficult decisions that come under the heading of rationing.

Conclusion

Although the ability of the medical profession to find new means of exerting its micro power should not be underestimated, and although the nature of the power balance between medicine and management is a complex and dynamic one, it does seem on reflection that the *Working for Patients* proposals marked an important watershed and turning point in the power play between these groups of stakeholders. More than Griffiths did, the Conservative Government's 1991 changes put several additional levers of power and persuasion into managers' hands. Moreover, the government looked to managers to implement the changes it wanted and resourced them to deliver accordingly. Unmistakably, the number, status, power and pay of senior NHS managers have grown. They may have suffered cuts in 1996, and be required to sustain yet more in future, but that does not negate the significant expansion of their numbers and the enhancement of their status and conditions of service which accompanied the 1991 changes.

Whatever the reality, and however unfair, central government and most managers are distrusted by NHS staff and public alike. They do not want a markedly different or privatized NHS, which is what they suspect was the Conservative government's real agenda, but an improved public one. This loss of trust between managers and policy-makers on the one hand and doctors on the other has manifested itself in a number of ways, including the mounting concern over rationing and calls for a government lead on how it might be made more rational. This pressure has also resulted from a parallel development which we consider in Chapter 4: namely, the arrival of a research and development (R&D) strategy in 1991 as part of the NHS changes and the related development of EBM. In addition to the battery of management tools, mentioned earlier, which are perceived as posing a threat to clinical autonomy, the R&D strategy can be seen as another mechanism aimed at challenging doctors' decisions and priorities and requiring them to account for their actions in cost-effective and outcomes terms. As we shall see in Chapter 4, so far, few managers have seized the potential in the R&D strategy and EBM approach for confronting doctors but it is certainly a government priority that they do so.

A third strand in the rationing debate has been the development of patient power and the growing desire for a greater public say in how priorities are set. The Patient's Charter has undoubtedly contributed to a new climate of patient influence, as has the criticism that the NHS is undemocratic – a victim of the so-called 'democratic deficit' (Stewart 1992) – and that health authorities are remote from the local communities they seek to serve. Such concerns have prompted proposals for rethinking local governance (Clarke, Hunter and Wistow 1995) and for actively giving the public a greater say in priorities. Both issues are taken up in Chapter 4.

In sum, not only are doctors increasingly reluctant to shoulder the burden of rationing at a time when the NHS changes, combined with allegedly acute resource pressures, have begun to force the issue of rationing into the public domain, by virtue of the purchaser–provider split and contract culture, but doctors' own practices are coming under closer scrutiny from two separate quarters: those in the scientific community, including some clinicians, who are questioning whether all that doctors do is efficacious and necessary since most of their practices have not been rigorously evaluated, and a more assertive, informed public who are being actively encouraged by the government to enter into a dialogue with their local health authorities in order to help shape local priorities.

In Chapter 4 we consider how rationing is being conducted by health authorities and the ways in which it is proposed that rationing decisions might be improved in future: namely, through a more research-based culture (centred on clinical effectiveness and EBM) on the one hand and by a more participatory decision-making process, in which the public is involved as a key stakeholder, on the other. We also consider the national–local tension and the calls on central government to give a lead on rationing and adopt an explicit approach to it.

CHAPTER 4

Rationing: a national or local matter?

Introduction

As Chapter 3 stated, up until the introduction of general management in the mid-1980s and the subsequent NHS changes in 1991, rationing decisions were largely left to the micro level, where doctors and patients come together and decisions are made to provide or withhold treatment or care. Central government set priorities nationally, which health authorities were required to follow and implement. But it was doctors' daily decisions which principally shaped policy and determined priorities and, for the most part, doctors were content to go along with and operate such a system. But, as Chapter 3 also demonstrated, the arrival of general management followed, a few years later, by the 1991 market-style reforms worked to change all this. In the process, fragile arrangements and understandings and intricate stratagems which had evolved over many decades were fatally disturbed or overturned. As a survey of Directors of Public Health reviewing the first three years of the NHS reforms concluded, the reforms 'are damaging the foundations of the system which they purported to improve' (Marks 1995: 1).

The management of the rationing problem was one of the arrangements which fell victim to the changes. And it was not long before calls came from various quarters for a more rational approach to rationing, notably from the medical profession and some (but by no means all) academic quarters. That those leading the calls could be accused of being rather naïve politically in no way served to deter them. As far as they were concerned rationality was on their side. They thought it illogical and irrational to allow rationing decisions to be reserved for local decision, and for there to be no explicit nationally agreed principles and frameworks to which local decision-makers could refer and be guided by. In a *national* health service, they argued, surely a national framework was a self-evident requirement. To believe or act otherwise was a blatant example of ministers evading their responsibilities to the public and, in Klein's words, indulging in 'blame diffusion' (Klein 1995). It was suggested that the experience of the approach to rationing adopted by the State of Oregon in the USA could serve as a model of how to approach the subject in an open and public way (see Chapter 5). Even those who were critical of the Oregon experiment, like the editor of the *British Medical Journal* (*BMJ*), Richard Smith, admired the manner in which a hitherto taboo subject had been brought out into the open and engaged the public. Smith (1991: 1562) believes that while it is tempting to leave decisions 'to be fudged by kindly professionals, I believe that we should follow the Oregonians into the sunlight'.

A national approach

One of the earliest calls for government to make explicit rationing decisions instead of looking to doctors to take them was from the British Medical Association at its 1992 conference. Its stance has subsequently been supported by a number of commentators, most vociferous among them being the editor of the *BMJ*, Richard Smith. He is a powerful advocate of the view that the UK needs a nationwide, prolonged, systematic debate on rationing and was highly critical of the Conservative government's refusal to be candid on rationing and even to use the term in ministers' public utterances. He wrote: 'This failure of leadership has meant that Britain has not had the broad, deep, informed, and prolonged debate on rationing that is needed' (Smith 1995: 686). Similar sentiments were expressed at a conference in July 1997 when the Labour Government was urged to grasp the nettle its predecessors had declined to do.

It is in fact hard to think of any major, and sensitive, public issue which has been debated in such a responsible manner. Why health-care rationing, a subject of extreme complexity, should be any different is therefore a little puzzling in the circumstances. The arguments surrounding the degree to which rationing should be explicit or implicit are the subject of the final chapter. Britain is also accused of lagging behind countries like The Netherlands, Sweden and New Zealand which, in different ways, have taken a national lead on rationing. Their experiences are reviewed in Chapter 5.

What international experience demonstrates, as well as the various endeavours in the UK to get ministers to take rationing seriously, is that there are several public approaches to tackling rationing, ranging from prescribed lists of treatments to be included in the NHS (akin to the Oregon experiment), through wide-ranging ethical discussions to establish criteria governing resource use (like the Dutch government's approach) to agreeing broad principles as the basis of a coherent policy framework. There is no consensus on the best way forward and the Conservative government resisted all attempts either to define a set of core services, to rank treatments, or to lead a public debate on the issue other than to reassert the founding principles of the NHS as a universal facility accessible to all in need of care and to reaffirm its view that it is for local health authorities not to ration care or deny effective treatments but to establish priorities informed by public opinion.

The reasons for the mounting pressure on the government to act more decisively have to do with a perception that difficult issues are being ducked – hard choices are not being made and certainly not in public.

One GP's opinion is typical: there is 'an unwillingness to face up to hard choices' (Cox 1995: 261). The belief among those of the 'hard choices' persuasion is that the government should come clean and lead a debate on how best to ration care in a publicly open, explicit manner.

To promote the debate, the advocates of such an approach – principally members of the Rationing Agenda Group (RAG), led by the *BMJ* and King's Fund (New 1996) – assert that within the NHS rationing is unavoidable because, even with more money, greater efficiency and better evidence about impact, 'one will always have to ask what the best uses are for the resources available, recognising that not everyone can have everything from which they could conceivably benefit' (Maxwell quoted in New 1996). RAG also maintains that health-care rationing – the need for it, how it is done, and whether the ways in which it is done are fair – should be more openly discussed and understood. Enhancing the quality of debate is a primary aim of the group. The group has not gone as far as to say that the public should be involved in the rationing of health care but it seems likely that some of its members would adopt this position. In the view of the group, rational rationing simply involves being more systematic, explicit and democratic.

In their analysis of rationing, New and Le Grand (1996) seek to marry features of the old implicit and clinician-led system with the need to be open and explicit about the principles governing rationing decisions. Their approach might be labelled 'principled pragmatism'. They suggest three basic characteristics that make some kinds of health care special: *unpredictability* of the need for that care, *information imbalance* between doctors and patients, and what might be termed the *fundamental importance* of the care concerned in allowing people to realize their life goals. The application of these principles (none of which would be sufficient on its own), argue their architects, might help in deciding what should be in the NHS and what should lie outside it. Some interventions are rather obvious and are already the subject of exclusions in some health authorities. Within their schema, New and Le Grand argue that cosmetic surgery to enhance physical attractiveness is not of fundamental importance and should not therefore be provided under the NHS. Other treatments or services are less obvious, such as residential care, which can be predicted. It should not therefore be available free under the NHS. But adult dental care and IVF should because both are unpredictable. Where New and Le Grand draw the line over being explicit and laying down fairly strict rules is over who should receive treatment and how much they should get. Pragmatism, they believe, should prevail here which means leaving such decisions to clinicians. What a national framework would achieve is an end to the present lottery whereby our place of residence can determine whether or not we have a chance of fertility treatment, continuing care, dentistry or whatever.

A difficulty with New and Le Grand's approach, beguiling though it is in its apparent simplicity, reasonableness and rationality, is how the characteristic of 'fundamental importance' is to be defined (Klein 1997). An illustration of the dilemma is provided by *in vitro* fertilization (IVF). Whereas New and Le Grand (1996: 52) assert its fundamental importance – 'is not the inability to have a child of fundamental importance?' – the Dunning Committee in The Netherlands which examined the whole issue of making choices in health care (see Chapter 5) excluded IVF from the basic package on the grounds that 'from a community-oriented approach, the answer to the question of necessity would most probably be no' (Ministry of Welfare, Health and Cultural Affairs 1992: 87).

This sharp divergence of view is precisely the point. When there exist multiple interpretations of what constitutes necessity or care of fundamental importance then it renders the whole selection criterion 'vacuous' since it 'provides no guidance on how conflicting interpretations can be resolved' (Klein 1997: 507).

For all their efforts to confront 'hard choices' in a hard-nosed fashion, New and Le Grand resort to an 'escape clause' and acknowledge the need for judgement since the three criteria of unpredictability, information imbalance and fundamental importance are not able 'to specify action so precisely that the need for further thought and judgement is unnecessary' (New and Le Grand 1996: 52). Individual cases will then need to be assessed so there can be no blanket exclusions. There is at the end of the day, it would seem, no substitute for clinical judgement and local discretion.

The Royal College of Physicians (RCP) (1995), in a move to bring about more public debate in making choices in health care and greater clarity in the process, has recommended the establishment of an independent National Council for Health Care Priorities. This would be largely expert in membership rather than representative but would include some public involvement. Such a body would review the methods for determining priorities at all levels within the NHS. Its aim would be:

to find ways and methods for improving priority setting in the NHS, bearing in mind the need to involve, educate and inform the public, the professions and the government. It would have the practical function of examining the evidence relating to resource allocation in health care, taking into account information from many sources; and it would review the basis and methods for determining allocations and their implications. Its role in society would be to identify all the relevant issues, analyse them publicly and comprehensively, and satisfy all interested parties that their views are being considered.

(Royal College of Physicians 1995: para. 4.28, 25)

The RCP believes that prevailing custom and practice leaves much to be desired because it is arbitrary, inconsistent and invariably covert. The College believes these flaws are a result of the absence of methods or guidelines, publicly aired and debated, to determine how decisions on priorities should be made. It is especially concerned at the inequity arising from discrimination against older people in access to curative treatments to which covert rationing can lead. Though it is condemned by the RCP, the government and the Medical Research Council, the practice continues to occur. The College is also anxious that the bodies responsible for setting priorities (health authorities and trusts) are primarily managerial rather than expert and are 'overwhelmingly subject to political and fiscal pressures inseparable from practical responsibilities for the management of restricted resources' (RCP 1995: para. 3.15, 17).

The College is not in favour of a Council or Commission (along the lines of that proposed by the Commission on Social Justice (1994)) which would devise legally enforceable rights to a guaranteed list of services. It is concerned that such a development would increase the potential for legal sanctions against doctors who, when making decisions, may for good reasons diverge from the intentions or requirements of a central directive. The Commission on Social Justice's proposal for a health-care guarantee, which would 'transform the moral right to treatment into a legally enforceable right', is aimed at 'reconciling health-care needs and health-care resources' (Commission on Social Justice 1994: 295). But a very precise health-care guarantee is neither straightforward to establish nor to implement and is open to all the limitations noted above in regard to New and Le Grand's schema.

The related idea of a National Council for Health Care Priorities has attracted considerable support from professional bodies, academic commentators and policy think-tanks. Klein (1995), while conceding the need for pragmatism, is critical of the 'half baked' variety which characterizes the British approach to muddling through. He states:

precisely because there is no way of resolving this question once and for all – because changing medical technical and shifting social attitudes will always create new dilemmas of choice – there is all the more reason for institutionalising what is bound to be a continuing debate.

(Klein 1995: 762)

But even Klein in his later writings on the subject acknowledges the limitations of a national approach. For example, he concedes that 'however much we may chafe at the way in which local discretion is often exercised, it still seems preferable to imposing a national template on the design and delivery of health care' (Klein 1997: 509). Later in the same article he concludes that 'we should accept the inevitability and indeed desirability of leaving rationing decisions to clinicians' and direct our efforts to making the process of decision-making more accountable.

The Institute for Public Policy Research (IPPR) has been one of the more active policy think-tanks when it comes to putting forward recommendations for making health-care rationing more rational. The Institute's position is quite clear. There has always been rationing in the NHS but the 1991 changes have made it more explicit. As a result, marked variations in the availability of treatments are evident in different localities thereby denying citizens equal access. Such a situation is iniquitous in a *national* health service. Therefore, the Institute wishes to see a rights-based framework put in place aimed at reconciling citizens' rights to appropriate health care with the need to manage scarce resources (Coote and Hunter 1996; Lenaghan 1996). The framework proposed includes the following components:

- national guidelines setting out criteria and procedures for rationing decisions in health care to guide decisions about who gets what
- a National Health Commission, to involve stakeholders in advising Parliament on national guidelines
- a *prima facie* right to appropriate health care on the basis of clinical need, with a right of appeal
- procedural rights to ensure fair dealing between patients and providers
- citizens' juries to involve the public in decisions
- explicit due process rights to fair treatment for those applying for and/or receiving NHS treatment and care
- enforcement by non-judicial means except as a last resort.

The rights-based approach's basic premise is that the NHS belongs to the people and is theirs by right. Thereafter, the following issues are important:

- it is a positive, not a negative approach based on what citizens can have rather than what they cannot have
- it facilitates equitable distribution since *all* citizens have rights
- it helps to establish certainty by setting out clear procedures and entitlements so that everyone knows where they stand
- by focusing on procedural rather than substantive rights and minimizing the role of the courts, it does not give rise to open-ended or unpredictable claims on public resources.

Substantive rights – amounting to a universal health-care guarantee of the kind proposed by the Commission on Social Justice – are not favoured because they risk introducing rigidities into the health-care system as well as committing governments to open-ended expenditure. They also put the individual before the collective and in the just distribution of resources a balance has to be struck between the individual and their needs together with those of the community as a whole. Procedural rights are more flexible and cost less to enforce. In favouring a national set of guidelines or Code of Practice which would provide a framework within which clinical discretion would operate, the Institute sees such a mechanism having two main functions (Lenaghan 1996: iii):

Firstly, it should redefine and clearly state the principles and purpose of the NHS. Secondly, it should set out the procedures and criteria by which decisions about rationing and resource allocation should be made. Local health authorities, trusts, clinicians and managers would abide by a shared set of rules. A framework of rights, set out in a Code of Practice, would ensure that each citizen has guaranteed access to a fair assessment procedure within the health service, based upon national principles which are open to public scrutiny and challenge.

Whether rationing should become a national matter or remain one for local resolution is a hotly contested subject (Lenaghan 1997a; Harrison 1997). It is also highly divisive not just between decision-making levels but also within them. Perhaps the question ought to be framed differently. It is not so much a matter of whether rationing *should* be subject to a nationally determined framework but whether it *can* be. Even if the 'should' question can be disposed of in the affirmative (and this is itself debatable), the 'can' question remains and, given the nature of the UK political and governmental system and its record of persistent policy failures, could represent a more formidable obstacle to overcome. A degree of realism may be salutary. Perhaps some issues or public policy dilemmas – those, as was suggested in the opening chapter, that are unwinnable – are so complex and difficult that any attempt to address them sensibly, or rationally in terms of central government leadership, only results in them becoming more entrenched and intractable. This may not in itself constitute a persuasive argument for not making the attempt to tackle them nationally. But, coupled with the government's poor record in providing sensible leadership in complex areas, it should alert us not to expect a satisfactory outcome and to warn us that what may result could prove far less satisfactory than what it seeks to replace. This is certainly not an argument in favour of the *status quo* because there are other options to be considered. Two of these are the subject of the next section: namely, the emphasis on knowledge-based decision-making and the greater involvement of the public locally through various means.

A local approach

Apart from a national rights-based approach and the call for a National Health Commission to prepare and agree national guidelines, which closely resembles the Royal College of Physicians' proposal for a National Council for Health Care Priorities, described above, there are other, primarily locally based, approaches which have been suggested. Some have even been tried. There is a division between those approaches which are dependent on what might be termed technocrats or the scientific community – notably health economists and health-services researchers – and those which endeavour to involve the public as active participants in the rationing process rather than as passive recipients of whatever is available or is offered. These two approaches are not mutually exclusive and could be seen as complementary but there is potentially a tension between the call to develop more scientific evidence through evidence-based medicine, and the desire to encourage greater public involvement in decisions about health-care provision (Hunter 1995a). In particular, what if the two approaches conflict as they do, for example, over hospital closures where the evidence in terms of location, safety, staffing and skill-mix among other factors may

Box 4.1 Health authorities' approaches to priority-setting

- Giving lower priority to costly new treatments of unproven effectiveness.

- Not purchasing those services traditionally available privately but not on the NHS.

- Not purchasing cosmetic techniques which even if desirable are not essential to health.

- Working with clinicians to develop methodologies for prioritizing care rather than excluding specific procedures.

- Taking a decision normally not to fund certain procedures.

- Limiting money available for certain services.

Source: Adapted from BMA 1995a: para. 26, 8.

all point convincingly to closure while public opinion stubbornly refuses to contemplate closure favouring instead keeping hospitals open? Can such divergent views, constituting as they do a 'political gap', be reconciled? Each of these approaches – the technocratic and the democratic – is considered in turn below. But first it is necessary to review the evidence, such as it is, about how rationing has been conducted by health authorities since the introduction of the NHS reforms in 1991.

Prevailing practice

Not a great deal is known about how health authorities have tackled the issue of rationing in their local settings. What knowledge there is of a more systematic and generalizable nature comes principally from four national surveys of health authorities carried out by the Centre for the Analysis of Social Policy at the University of Bath, conducted between 1992 and 1996, and published by NAHAT (Klein and Redmayne 1992; Redmayne, Klein and Day 1993; Redmayne 1995, 1996). A summary and overview of all four surveys is provided in Klein, Day and Redmayne (1996). The House of Commons Health Committee collected evidence for its study of priority-setting in 1995 and examples of the approaches taken by health authorities are listed in Box 4.1. There is also the study of priority-setting for health gain in six district health authorities carried out by Ham and colleagues (Ham, Honigsbaum and Thompson 1993).

A number of features arising from local priority-setting or rationing merit comment. First, there is the sheer diversity of local practice and the documents and plans providing a framework or structure for this. There is no common or standardized approach which makes systematic inter-authority comparisons virtually impossible. There are no common baseline data provided and therefore no means of comparing like with like.

Box 4.2 Examples of services not normally purchased

- Tattoo removal.

- Reversal of sterilization/vasectomy.

- Assisted conception.

- Gender-reassignment surgery.

- Breast augmentation/reduction.

- Radial keratotomy.

- Homeopathy/osteopathy/chiropractice/acupuncture.

- Treatment of bat ears in children.

- Treatment of non-genital warts.

Source: BMA 1995a: para. 27, 8.

Some health authorities have sought to exclude selected treatments: about one-quarter of the 100 health authorities in England explicitly identified in their 1996–97 purchasing plans procedures to be excluded from their contracts (Klein 1997). Not surprisingly, the exclusions are dominated by various forms of cosmetic surgery ranging from tattoo removal to buttock lift, from breast augmentation to bat ears (see Box 4.2). Some health authorities have also begun to exclude procedures like dilatation and curettage (D&C) for women under 40 where the evidence raises doubts about their clinical effectiveness. Purchasers have been influenced in part by the publication of the series of *Effective Health Care* bulletins, produced by Leeds and York Universities, which advise on how to purchase health care as effectively as possible within the constraints of the knowledge base.

The central point about all these efforts is that, as Klein puts it, they affect 'only the small change of NHS activity' (Klein 1997: 508). Such 'nibbling at the edges' is both inevitable and evidence of the flawed nature of an approach which seeks to exclude treatments and restrict the NHS menu. The heterogeneous nature of patients and their variable needs makes it all but impossible to operate successfully a policy of blanket exclusions. Therefore, most health authorities have adopted a more pragmatic, flexible stance whereby if a clinical need can be demonstrated then it will be met.

If it is difficult enough to make progress at the margins of what might be termed mainstream medicine, the prospect of what reaction might be forthcoming if health authorities moved in on what were seen as core activities is just too awful a prospect for health authorities even to contemplate. So, for the most part, they simply do not. Moreover, the issue of exclusions is seen as a diversionary sideshow – a fringe activity – while the main issues remain to be addressed: namely, not whether to provide a service but rather how much to provide, to whom and how to provide it. To focus discussion on exclusions or lists or menus will always confine the debate to marginal issues while the effective management of mainstream medicine will go unchallenged. In essence, the real challenge of rationing is finding some accommodation between a patient's needs and circumstances and the resources available at a particular point in time. Judgement is a critical feature of the many daily decisions which are made about finding just such an accommodation or fit between the ideal on the one hand and the acceptable on the other. In such a dynamic, ever-shifting landscape it becomes almost impossible sensibly to have an explicit and publicly sustainable approach to rationing. But this is not to deny that improvements in decision-making are needed. It is to meet this objective that knowledge-based medicine has become a key priority for health authorities as well as finding new ways of involving the public in priority-setting.

From the Bath surveys of priority-setting, it would seem that little has fundamentally changed from the studies of decision-making and priority-setting following the 1974 NHS reorganization (see, for example, Haywood and Alaszewski 1980; Hunter 1980; Ham 1981). These and other studies portrayed a local decision-making process and culture within the NHS as one of managerial coping, with little serious attention being paid to the implementation of national priorities. While problems were tackled, they were not solved. As Hunter (1980: 183) put it, decision-making consisted 'largely of administering and maintaining a system rather than of making fundamental changes in it'. In allocating development funds, 'the general rule governing [their] allocation was that "something is better than nothing". A policy of appeasement was preferred, the aim being to keep as many people happy as possible' (Hunter 1980: 188).

Some 20 years on, things do not appear markedly different. The stratagem adopted by many health authorities surveyed by the Bath team was to spread resources around, trying to do a little of everything to keep the pressure groups quiet rather than making significant changes. In the circumstances it was a perfectly rational response. Moreover, as the work of Klein and his colleagues shows, acute services still receive priority despite mental health services figuring prominently in health authorities' top 10 priorities – they received 17 per cent of priority development funds compared with 85 per cent for acute services (Klein, Day and Redmayne 1996). Even when priority services received funding it was modest and in some cases only of symbolic importance. Priority statements, then, appear to be at the level of aspiration rather than real intent and this pattern has been a feature of the NHS since the first systematic and explicit attempt to establish priorities in the mid-1970s.

Despite attempts to ration explicitly in respect of the marginal procedures noted earlier, the most favoured strategy for restricting access to health care is to leave decision-making to clinicians while seeking to improve its knowledge base through the development and application of guidelines and protocols (Redmayne 1995). A more recent trawl of health authorities' purchasing plans for 1997–98, by a consulting firm Blackwell Masters, shows that out of 120 plans 48 are seeking to disinvest in treatments considered to be of marginal value or cost-effectiveness (*Guardian* G2 Section 1997: 11). But it is one thing to write such restrictions into plans and another entirely to implement them. Time will tell.

Some health authorities have sought to 'break the mould' by adopting innovative approaches to priority-setting/rationing. One such initiative is the simulation exercise undertaken by the Southampton and South West Hampshire Health Commission in 1991. The exercise was then followed up in 1994 and has been documented in a study by Honigsbaum, Richards and Lockett (1995a). The authors acknowledge the complexity and messiness of priority-setting and concede there are no easy or correct solutions. A number of lessons emerged from the 'Purchasing Dilemmas' exercise. For all the investment in sophisticated ranking and priority-setting devices, such as cost-utility analysis and programme budgeting, at the end of the process value judgements, 'guesstimates' and 'gut feelings' were probably the main determinants of the choices made. The Southampton experiment sought to combine two utilitarian approaches: the first based on cost-effectiveness principles, i.e. health-care resources should be allocated in proportion to anticipated benefits weighed against costs, and the second based on allowing the public to decide how spending priorities should be established. Both approaches accept that the 'collective benefit of the majority can trump the rights of the individual' (Doyal 1995: 83–4). We go on to consider these two approaches in greater detail. Before doing so, it is worth drawing attention to a paradox: at the same time as utilitarian approaches emphasizing the maximization of benefits for the many over the few are in the ascendant, so is the notion of consumerism with its stress on the individual. There is a structural conflict between these approaches which is probably irreconcilable. As Doyal (1995: 82) says, 'We cannot have it both ways.'

The technocratic approach

One approach favoured by some commentators and analysts is the development of a basic health-care package or guaranteed entitlement to a package of core services with lists of what treatments are included and excluded. This approach has been tried in other countries (see Chapter 5), albeit without much success (Lenaghan (ed) 1997b). Although it has been suggested in the UK by, for example, National Economic Research Associates (NERA) (1994) and the Healthcare 2000 group

(Healthcare 2000 1995), it has not attracted a great deal of support. Indeed, the approach has come in for considerable criticism on the grounds that it would reduce flexibility to provide appropriate care to individuals and to adapt to changing circumstances (Coote and Hunter 1996; Lenaghan 1996). Moreover, no matter how generously the basic package is defined it is likely to be seen by the public as a way of cutting back services and restricting access to health care. It could hasten the departure of the middle classes from the NHS to the private sector, thereby beginning the process where the NHS becomes a residual service for the poor and chronic sick. If the articulate, assertive higher income groups exited from the NHS the fear would be that there would no longer be pressure for maintaining quality of service or raising standards. In countries which have attempted to define a basic package, almost all treatments end up being included because politically it is very difficult to be unequivocal about excluding anything. It also seems clear that one of the motives of advocates of a guaranteed entitlement to health care, like NERA and Healthcare 2000, is to encourage the development of a competitive market in private health-care insurance.

Further manifestations of the technocratic rational approach are the various techniques which are available to aid priority-setting or rationing. Probably best known among these is the quality adjusted life year (QALY) methodology (Williams 1985). Health economists are concerned not merely with the effectiveness of treatments but with their cost-effectiveness. The QALY approach attempts to evaluate healthcare outcomes according to a generic scale. It asks (a) to what extent, and for how long, will a treatment improve the quality of a patient's life, and (b) how much does the treatment cost? If the improvement in health after treatment is both significant and long-lasting, the patient accumulates units and scores high on the quality-of-life measure. If the treatment is relatively expensive, then the cost per unit of quality is low. The theory favours treatments which achieve the greatest in the quality of life, over the longest period, for the least cost. The adoption of health policies which produce the largest number of QALYs will be those which spend money most efficiently. Economists differ over how far QALYs should be the determinant of decisions. Many would see them as doing no more than informing decisions on priorities rather than deciding them.

Despite the considerable interest QALYs have attracted, the scheme has had little practical impact. Health-service managers frequently, and almost without exception, express interest in the idea at a theoretical or conceptual level but it has not modified their practices or priorities in notable ways. The Southampton experiment cited earlier is a good example of the limitations of QALYs and similar techniques although, to be fair, the reliability of the measures and data, and their non-availability in some cases, left much to be desired. This prompted Robinson (1995: 75) to warn of 'the mismatch between expectations

Box 4.3 Problems with QALYs

- When using QALYs, it is necessary to clarify the nature of the margin that is being used for comparison. In particular, are we comparing treatment X with treatment Y, or with no treatment at all? What kind of population are we considering extending treatment to, and are they more, or less, clinically suitable than those patients already in receipt of it? (Mooney *et al.* 1992; Drummond, Torrance and Mason 1993; Gerrard and Mooney 1993).

- Is the context of the QALY study transferable to that of the decision-maker? Results obtained by doctors in one location may not be matched elsewhere because of differences between doctors, patients and facilities. Costs may also differ widely between locations. International comparisons should be treated with special caution (Gerrard and Mooney 1993).

- How comparable are the cost bases of different QALY studies? Do they just include health agencies' costs or are they broader? (Drummond, Torrance and Mason 1993; Gerrard and Mooney 1993).

- What is the empirical base of the utility weightings which define the relative quality of life? Several studies have been based on non-random samples of less than 100 respondents.

- Has account been taken of the tendency of respondents to give different values to unadjusted years of life at different ages? (Gafni and Birch 1991).

Source: Harrison and Hunter 1994: 48.

based upon theory and the reality of practice which threatens to discredit economic evaluation'.

As a rationing device, QALYs assume that resources will be allocated in accordance with capacity to benefit from their use. Health gain arises from the most cost-effective application of these resources. According to Le Grand (quoted in Gormally 1996: 5), 'If health care is rationed according to the cost per unit of health gain, such that treatments with lower costs per unit are given priority over those with higher costs, then more health gain in total will be achieved from a given set of resources.'

QALYs, and cost-utility analysis more generally, have come in for considerable criticism largely on ethical and moral grounds since such techniques place undue emphasis on community well-being at the expense of individual well-being. In this respect QALYs are seen to be ruthlessly, and possibly unacceptably, utilitarian. QALYs are also criticized for discriminating against elderly people and those with disabilities. Harrison and Hunter (1994) list a number of caveats about putting QALYs into operation (see Box 4.3).

These technical problems and limitations of QALYs should not be lightly dismissed. Robinson (1995) points to the concern among economists themselves about the poor quality of data and methods used, about the difficulties of comparing studies undertaken in different years, and of using different measures of costs and benefits. He concludes: 'There are simply too many gaps in our knowledge at the moment to be able to rely on extant evidence as a basis for decision-making.' More problematic is the ability of QALYs to conceal ethical and political judgements within a formula which appears scientific and therefore 'objective' and 'true' (Coote and Hunter 1996: 59). As Carr-Hill (1991: 360) wryly observes, 'This century's history of the attempt to claim that all value conflicts can be resolved within a technical framework is, of course, long and distinguished.' Carr-Hill, himself an economist, is suspicious of the technocratic approach which the QALY methodology embodies and its implications for democratic accountability and discussions about priorities. 'The introduction of a half-understood technical device will only serve to mystify and obfuscate these discussions and remove them further from democratic control' (Carr-Hill 1991: 361).

A key criticism of the cost-utility technique is whether it is feasible to collapse the multifaceted phenomena of life and its quality on to a single valid scale. In sum, the costs-per-QALY approach 'wraps up into an ostensibly technical formula a variety of ethical and political judgements to which we may or may not subscribe' (Harrison and Hunter 1994: 50). Mooney *et al.* (1992) concede that QALYs suffer from a number of theoretical and practical drawbacks. For instance, they do not deal very well with health-care objectives such as equity. Also, adequate outcome data are currently scarce or non-existent. QALYs do not deal at all with non-health outputs such as information and reassurance received from professional carers.

The most fundamental objection to QALYs lies in the attempt to devise a common measure by which we can assign a quantitative value to disparate ingredient factors in quality of life (Gormally 1996: 5). They are incommensurable. Loughlin (1996) makes the same point when he argues that the QALY device is very 'accommodating' to those who want to make priority-setting seem more rational since 'In addition to its bogus objectivity it successfully disguises the incommensurability of many of the values involved in decisions about the allocation of health resources.' More fundamentally, Loughlin asserts that the advocates of the QALY are colluding with those who subscribe to things as they are rather than as how they could be. He accuses them of being conservative in outlook and accepting of the present state of 'semi-barbarism' which passes for society. He rejects the assumption that there must be a defensible answer to questions about who should be allowed to suffer and die. Referring to rationing and old age, Loughlin (1996: 155) claims that

not only is it not obvious that we can find an acceptable rational answer to the question: 'should the elderly ... be sacrificed, for the sake of the very young?', the very idea that we *can* do so is offensive nonsense, and the attempt to construct devices or principles which enable people to make such decisions 'ethically' is an attempt to make nonsense of ethics.

Le Grand offers the notion of 'moral intuition' as a defence against unacceptable and inequitable rationing principles. Their outcomes, he asserts, should not be morally offensive about what is considered equitable. But Gormally finds reliance on moral intuition in a pluralistic society quite inadequate. In such a society, 'everyone's wants are apt to be given the rhetorical status of "rights" [which] merely invites the interminable contesting of whatever rationing decisions invoke intuition as their justification' (Gormally 1996: 6). Doyal also pursues the critique of QALYs on moral grounds. QALYs, he asserts, clearly value some individuals (e.g. children) over others (e.g. elderly people). In his view, 'such a principle of inequality challenges the moral fabric of our society – the belief in the equality of humans' (Doyal 1995: 84).

We return to these matters in the final chapter when considering the issue of how far rationing should be an explicit or implicit process. Meantime, let us return to the attempts by economists and others to find acceptable solutions to the dilemma of making choices. Proponents of QALYs are not alone in attempting to evaluate health outcomes on the basis of economics. We need not detail all the tools available here (see Mooney *et al.* 1992 for a useful and succinct summary of these). It is sufficient for our purposes to echo Newdick's (1995: 26) caution when he argues that 'There are reasons . . . for doubting whether any outcome measure . . . will be able to do more than provide general support for decisions which have already been made on other grounds.'

Moreover, whatever the value of economic devices like QALYs at the level of macro allocation, they are likely to be too blunt and one-dimensional to guide those who must distinguish between patients in need of treatment. As Robinson (1995: 231) warns, 'There is a real danger that the current headlong drive to include considerations of cost-effectiveness in health policy decision-making will lead to a serious backlash if health economists fail to meet the expectations being placed upon them.'

Similar reservations underlie the evidence-based medicine (EBM) movement which is also gathering pace in the UK with an impressive evidence-based complex or industry now in place following a period of rapid expansion since 1991 (Appleby, Walshe and Ham 1995) (see Box 4.4). Rather like health economists, though lacking their status and pre-eminence, health-services researchers are joining the army of technocrats armed with government grants and contracts to come up with 'scientific' methodologies and solutions to intractable political problems. The rise of the EBM movement is a good example of this process at work. In the words of Carr-Hill (1995: 1467): 'Welcome? To the brave new world of evidence-based medicine.'

The drive towards an evidence-based health service began with the arrival of the NHS Research and Development strategy in 1991. The post of Director of R&D was created in 1990 in response to the House of Lords Select Committee report, *Priorities for Medical Research* (House of Lords Select Committee on Science and Technology 1988).

Box 4.4 Evidence-based complex

- Health-technology assessment programme.

- NHS Centre for Reviews and Dissemination.

- *Effective Health Care* bulletins.

- UK Cochrane Centre/Collaboration.

- UK Clearing House on Health Outcomes.

- National Clinical Audit Information and Dissemination Centre.

- Central Health Outcomes Unit.

- Centre for Evidence-Based Medicine.

The Director of R&D is responsible for advising the Secretary of State for Health on all research matters. The NHS R&D strategy aims to create a knowledge-based health service in which clinical, managerial and policy decisions are based on sound information about research findings and scientific developments. The first Director of R&D, Michael Peckham, stated that the programme is based on several key points (Peckham 1991). First, R&D is a prerequisite for achieving a cost-effective health service. Second, investment in R&D is essential to establish a substantial and coherent research programme. Peckham claims that the NHS R&D initiative is probably 'the first comprehensive attempt to develop a national R&D infrastructure for health care . . . [It] offers a unique opportunity to develop an overall view of basic and applied research in relation to health care and health priorities' (Peckham 1991: 371). While the profile of health research has undoubtedly been raised as a result of the NHS R&D initiative, its ability to deliver an improved health service and better informed health policy remains unproven. This is not a criticism since it will be many years before the initiative can be expected to bear fruit. However, there are many who are anxious to see quick results. They are likely to be disappointed.

The NHS R&D strategy has spawned a new industry in the evaluation of health care and the production of information about the effectiveness of various interventions. The evidence-based complex, already mentioned, has taken the form of several new academic research centres and projects producing information aimed at policy-makers, managers and practitioners as well as a host of new publications aimed at the research community and at those managing and providing health care.

Very quickly, the NHS R&D initiative became imbued with the language of clinical effectiveness and evidence-based medicine. Indeed, one of the NHS Executive's six national medium-term priorities for

1997–98 centres on EBM and effectiveness issues involving the production and application of clinical guidelines and protocols (NHS Executive 1996).

It is sometimes forgotten that the R&D strategy has two components: research *and* development. Invariably, attention is focused on the former but the second component – development – is, perhaps a little belatedly, slowly being seen as of equal importance especially in areas where the problem is not lack of research evidence *per se* but an inability to act on the evidence available. The failure is one of implementation. Generating high quality data is of little value in itself unless these are transformed into useful information which modify, if necessary, clinical and/or other behaviour. Hence the focus of the R&D strategy is shifting towards getting research through development and into practice. As Sackett and Rosenberg (1995: 249) put it: 'The issue is no longer how little of medical practice has a firm basis in such evidence; the issue today is how much of what is firmly based is actually applied in the front lines of patient care.'

Apart from the structures and priorities of the NHS R&D programme, and its offshoots clinical effectiveness and EBM, interest in these developments has centred on two related concerns: first, how realistic is it to expect EBM to move clinicians from opinion-based practice towards knowledge-based medicine; and, second, how far is EBM a solution to the rationing problem, the assumption here being that if sufficient resources can be released from areas of demonstrable ineffectiveness then this will surely offset the need to ration care. After all, it is hardly a matter of rationing if patients are being denied ineffective and/or unsafe procedures. Self-evidently, they should not be available at all. In short, what scope exists for making rationing rational and is this an acceptable role for, and set of expectations to have of, EBM?

The first point concerns the ability of EBM to deliver solutions to the problem as conceived by policy-makers and managers: namely, what works and does not work in medicine. Providing intelligence for rational decision-making is a laudable goal but how achievable is it in practice? Arguably, to regard EBM as a panacea for solving the problems of resource constraints and rationing is misconceived and would appear to fly in the face of the history of the NHS during its first 50 years or so.

It is necessary to take a step back and pay closer attention to how research is perceived, and subsequently used or rejected, by those at whom it is aimed. Those who subscribe to research as a rational, scientific process, and who thereby ignore its knowledge base and the politics of this, are deluding themselves if they believe that there exists a linear progression from research findings to implementation (Hunter 1995b). There is a prior need to understand the sociological and political contexts in which research is conducted and to which its findings are subsequently applied. Policy-makers who advocate changing the behaviour of clinicians and others as a solution to the problem they

Box 4.5 Barriers to clinical effectiveness

- Clinical practice is uncertain.

- Clinical effectiveness is one issue on a crowded agenda for doctors and managers.

- Financial dimension discourages the culture of effectiveness – seen as an exercise in cost-cutting.

- Doctors deal with individuals, not populations.

- Clinical effectiveness is complex and takes time to achieve.

- Managers lack confidence (and possibly legitimacy) in dealing with clinical issues.

- Risk of information overload.

- Clinical effectiveness seen as a top–down process – local ownership is weak.

Source: Sheldon and Long (1994).

perceive as the inappropriate use of health-care services, without first considering provider motives, risk losing the support of providers and putting in jeopardy the whole effectiveness policy (Grogan *et al.* 1994).

The drive for clinical effectiveness now permeates the NHS at the level of rhetorical aspiration, though few examples exist of successful attempts to promote it. Clinical guidelines may be in high fashion but professional resistance to their introduction remains a problem and the extent to which they will change clinical behaviour is uncertain. A range of barriers to the implementation of clinical effectiveness has been identified (Sheldon and Long 1994) and a list of the principal ones is given in Box 4.5. Cumulatively, these amount to a formidable set of obstacles to be overcome or negotiated.

Few studies exist which seek to illuminate the 'black box' of medical decision-making and the processes of knowing and acting. An exception is a small study by Tanenbaum (1994) in which she explores two approaches to medical problem-solving: deterministic and probabilistic. On the one hand, deterministic reasoning searches out the causes and mechanisms of illness, therapy and action; on the other hand, probabilistic reasoning draws on what past experience predicts. Effectiveness, including outcomes, research is intended to improve medical care by improving clinicians' practice and increasing their stock of probabilistic knowledge.

Tanenbaum found that clinicians for the most part rely on personal experience over research data. They are realists rather than empiricists. Effectiveness research is considered useful but only as one of many forms of knowledge which can influence a decision or course of action.

On the basis of this finding, Tanenbaum asserts that doctors act as they do for good reason and that the uncertain and complex nature of medical work is a determinant of their bias towards decision-making based on experience and judgement rather than on probabilities. The clinicians she studied acted interpretively and intuitively by making sense of the problem confronting them within its particular context. Virtually every member of her sample referred to the sheer volume and complexity of clinical information. This is then filtered through the 'vast and idiosyncratic' knowledge bank which each clinician accumulates.

Even among clinicians who endorse effectiveness research, deterministic knowledge derived from contact with each individual and unique patient cannot be ruled out. Such an approach may be perfectly rational and defensible, for it is rarely possible to be conclusive about the total ineffectiveness of a particular intervention for everyone who might benefit from it. For instance, a very elderly patient may benefit from a kidney transplant in terms of having five years or more of good quality life ahead of her. Yet most governments, if not managers and some clinicians, are likely to subscribe to a notional age limit or threshold which would preclude allocating resources to such an intervention in a person of advanced age. Even in the UK, where age as a rationing criterion is formally outlawed, the practice is widespread. In such cases, which, as was noted in Chapter 2, are common in discussions of rationing, the balancing of the generalized knowledge base (e.g. the availability of kidney transplants in patients of advanced age) with the particular (i.e. what would work for *this* patient) becomes the central issue. Probabilism is not well suited to caring for individuals.

Decision-making becomes an iterative process embracing patient, intervention and effectiveness/outcome variables from which a decision is arrived at. The process is akin to notions in organization theory of 'bounded rationality' and 'satisficing' propounded by Simon (1957). Since there are cognitive limits to rationality, these notions, which constitute a sort of rationality, account more precisely for the way in which decisions are reached in practice.

Effectiveness research, therefore, cannot be isolated from its social and political setting. Nor do clinicians appear to do so. They are convinced that such research, and the heavy 'marketing' of it, is linked directly to policy-makers' desire to contain or reduce costs rather than enhance the quality of health care. Even those doctors who, in Tanenbaum's sample, held positive views of effectiveness research did not believe it would fundamentally alter their practice or clinical medicine in general. It was merely another intrusion to be negotiated or bypassed. In Tanenbaum's (1994: 39) words, doctors 'were grappling with real discontinuities – between probability and the treatment of individual patients, between the usefulness of outcomes data and the claims being made for them'. It would appear, then, that not only are research findings enlisted to serve political purposes but that they are also perceived within a political context by those at whom they are aimed.

What is happening in the arena of effectiveness research is, in part at least, a political power struggle between clinicians on the one hand and a newly empowered breed of health-services researchers on the other embracing a range of disciplines but principally epidemiology, statistics and health economics. The authority and influence of this group are in the ascendancy. Clinicians who, for the most part, have practised their craft unchallenged are now being actively challenged and made to account for their actions. Such developments have not gone so far as to pose a real threat to the prevailing power structure and they may never be allowed to. Nonetheless, the perception is that clinicians' autonomy is under threat and cannot survive the increasingly strong scientific base to medical practice (Walker 1997). Concern over such a development might not be so great if there was not so much scepticism about the prescriptive rigour of effectiveness research. Medicine *is* inherently uncertain and its art and craft dimensions, including the exercise of what Vickers (1965) has termed 'appreciative judgement', cannot be lightly dismissed or overlooked. The search for certainty in such a context is destined for disappointment (Klein 1996).

These considerations are of central importance when it comes to the second reason offered for the enthusiastic reception which has greeted EBM from policy-makers (including ministers) and managers who see it as a solution (or partial solution) to the rationing dilemma. The new scientism is seen to be the principal means through which ineffective procedures can be eliminated thereby making it unnecessary, or reducing the extent of the need, to make difficult choices, i.e. ration health care. It is an attractive, beguiling position to adopt especially as it obscures or conceals the political, value basis of decisions beneath a veneer of scientific certainty and rationality. Essentially political questions and choices become transformed into technical ones which nicely lets politicians and managers 'off the hook'. They can take shelter behind the evidence which, they will opine, has been objectively and independently assembled. As Klein claims, 'The new scientism appears to offer politicians less pain, less responsibility for taking difficult decisions and a legitimate way of curbing what are often seen as the idiosyncratic and extravagant practices of doctors' (Klein 1996: 85). Moreover, as noted above, there is a risk that as EBM becomes embedded, those researchers concerned with effectiveness and outcomes issues will become the arbiters of what constitutes appropriate evidence. As Morone (1993: 735) states, arguments over who controls outcomes research are part of a much larger conflict, namely, 'the effort to re-shape the practice of medicine from outside the profession'.

But the danger in all this does not lie only, or even principally, with the scientific community. Its practitioners, or at least those who are not carried away by their own zeal and sense of mission, may be careful to stress the limitations of their science and the need for it to be seen as only one input among many in the decision process. As Klein (1996) points out, 'The real danger is rather different: that a vulgarised form of the new scientism will be taken up by ministers and managers – and that their eventual disillusionment will lead to a disproportionate reaction.'

Little is to be gained by 'the imposition of a spurious rationality on an inherently irrational process' (McKee and Clarke 1995). Similar points have been made by Carr-Hill (1995) in his critique of EBM and, in particular, its methodological bias in favour of randomized control trials despite the strengths and greater sensitivity of other methods. 'You only needed a standard patient, a standard treatment and a standard outcome to be a researcher' (p. 1468) which, of course, does violence to reality. Carr-Hill warns of the dangers of devaluing complexity and denying context and therefore of marginalizing the role of judgement in decision-making.

Above all, there is a need to remain modest in any expectations of EBM. At best it will better inform rationing decisions but it is not a panacea for difficult and ultimately value-based judgements on what to provide or deny patients. Moreover, EBM risks seeing 'reality' as consisting only of phenomena that can be quantified and measured (Frankford 1994). If judgement in health care is to be accorded its rightful place then EBM carries no easy solutions to the difficult calculus involved in rationing or funding decisions. Even where EBM is part of the culture of health care it is unlikely that the exercise of choice can be avoided. Rationing, within the prevailing political and social parameters, is therefore probably inevitable. What the advocates of EBM usefully remind us of is that even if rationing is necessary we should at least be as certain as we can reasonably be that treatments EBM tells us are ineffective are not provided or only in exceptional cases where capacity to benefit is demonstrated (Hunter 1996a, 1996b). But, to sound a note of caution, the task will not be an easy one for the reasons Eddy cites (1994: 328):

Studies of variations in practice patterns, inappropriate care, physician uncertainty, and the lack of good evidence of effectiveness for many practices suggest that there is a lot of waste. But that does not mean the job of finding and eliminating waste will be easy . . . [T]he existence of waste will not eliminate the tough decisions, or the need to ration.

So far we have considered EBM from the perspective of care providers and the problems arising from its practical application to clinical decision-making. But there is a further dimension to be considered in an assessment of EBM which concerns the *relevance* of the evidence produced by the R&D initiative for purchasers. For the most part, according to Gray, Bevan and Frankel (1997), evidence is of low importance for purchasers. An explanation lies in the regulatory framework within which purchasers operate. Focused as it is on the efficiency index and *Patient's Charter*, evidence is seen as irrelevant. As Gray, Bevan and Frankel (1997: 8) recommend, 'It would be helpful if regulation were developed which used evidence to derive measures of effectiveness, appropriateness and efficiency.' In this way R&D would be seen as central to purchasing instead of as being marginal to it – 'an optional indulgence for enlightened purchasers'.

Gray, Bevan and Frankel's analysis of the absence of an R&D culture among purchasers is supported by the findings of a survey of purchasers and clinical effectiveness and EBM (Walshe and Ham 1997). The study found that while clinical effectiveness figured on the agendas of most health authorities (and also trust boards) it was far from being a regular, formal part of their discussions. The researchers reach similar conclusions to those of Gray, Bevan and Frankel. Evidence-based purchasing will not be realized unless and until health authorities' performance is measured according to effectiveness criteria. But what Gray, Bevan and Frankel, and Walshe and Ham fail to consider is that purchasers' reluctance or failure to embrace EBM may in part be caused by the complexities involved, the contested nature of the evidence in some cases, and the enormous difficulties encountered in translating aggregated data derived from randomized control trials into specific services for individuals.

Various initiatives are underway to support knowledge-based decision-making but they are not cost-free which must be an issue of some concern at a time when management costs are being squeezed. For instance, one such initiative is the Getting Research into Practice and Purchasing (GRiPP) project initiated by the former Oxford RHA in 1993. The project has four main aims: to identify and undertake the steps involved in using research evidence to change clinical practice; to examine the role of commissioning authorities and contracting in this process; to document and share the lessons learned from the project; and to involve patients and the public in the process (Appleby, Walshe and Ham 1995). Key lessons from the project are listed in Box 4.6. One of these is the time and effort it all takes and these no longer come cheap in the NHS. An issue must be how realistic it is to expect such an approach to be replicated across the country. Moreover, how can we be sure that the investment will be outweighed by the anticipated benefits?

Whatever the strengths and limitations of EBM, for all the various stakeholders, what is not in doubt is that the rationing issue, if handled as a solely technical problem, will not lead to open, public debate about what are at root value-based decisions. Indeed, it could actually inhibit public debate and lead to decisions being taken in wholly unaccountable ways on the grounds that they are technical matters beyond the public's grasp. The illusion of technical precision could effectively stifle political debate and depoliticize matters of intense political importance (Hunter 1995a: 882). This would constitute a major policy paradox if it has any salience since another of the government's medium-term priorities is the active engagement of the public in decisions about priorities. It is also another utilitarian justification for discriminatory rationing with all the moral dilemmas that gives rise to (Doyal 1995). We now turn to this topic.

Box 4.6 Key lessons from participants in the GRiPP project (GRiPP 1994)

- Both **nationally available research evidence** and a clear, robust and local justification for change are needed in order to secure support.

- **Consultation and involvement** of interested parties, preferably led by a respected product champion, needs to be thorough and comprehensive.

- **Change in one sector**, such as acute care, can have major consequences for others, such as general practice and primary care, which need to be addressed and taken into account.

- Access to **information about current practice and the effects of change** is very important but that information is not usually available from routine data systems.

- **Contracts are best used to summarize discussion and agreement** that has taken place elsewhere, not as a focus for discussion and debate.

- **Costing the changes in practice** may reveal that more effective care costs more, not less. In any case, costing is unlikely to result in the release of resources or financial savings, though it may release capacity for other purposes.

- The process requires **good, constructive relationships between providers and purchasers** if change is to be achieved.

- **It all takes much more time than might be expected.** Even implementing a single initiative requires a substantial commitment of local time and effort, and the availability of appropriate clinical and research skills.

Source: Appleby, Walshe and Ham (1995).

The participative approach

The public have a dual relationship with the NHS: as patients (or customers) and as citizens (members of society). As patients they have an immediate interest in what happens to them as individuals as and when they use services. As citizens they have a more general interest in what happens to them as part of the wider community. These two interests, or roles, might well conflict – not least when decisions have to be made about allocating finite resources. Patient power, at the level of the individual user of services, must go hand-in-hand with public accountability even if there is a tension between them. Coote (1993: 37) has sought to make a distinction between the two roles:

Generally, it can be said that members of the public relate to micro-level decisions as customers and to macro-level decisions as citizens (although the distinction is often blurred). It could be said that decisions about rationing are a matter for the public as citizens, rather than as customers. This is because they are bound to affect not just one individual but the community as a whole.

In reality, rationing decisions cut across the micro and macro levels although what may be appropriate at the micro level for the individual may not be appropriate at the macro level as far as the community is concerned. Reconciling these differences, and determining whether both levels should be open to public scrutiny or only the macro level (micro level decisions being best left to the patient and their doctor), are difficult matters which have not been satisfactorily resolved. In the remainder of this section, the focus is on the citizen operating at an intermediate level between the macro and micro, i.e. the meso level: the level of the local community.

Public involvement in decisions is regarded as an important element in the rationing debate. Yet while it is easy at a rhetorical or symbolic level to sing the praises of the public being involved in consensus-building about the scope of health care, its practical achievement is considerably more difficult. It is also likely to be expensive both in human and financial resources. Moreover, it is by no means self-evident that the public as a whole wishes to be empowered in this way. In any case, what is this thing called 'the public'? Surely there is no single monolithic or uniform public but rather several publics each with its own particular values and preferences. Can there then be a consensus or one that is of any practical value?

So far efforts to involve the public in making choices about health care have had only limited success. As Moore (1996: 15) explains: 'Nationally, "public debate" ends up as media debate, when issues are inevitably treated in a simplistic way. Locally, purchasers have sometimes met with apathy when attempting to debate general principles, while moves to restrict or close services typically prompt vocal opposition.' In addition, 'asking the general public to weigh up the merits of different demands can produce results which conflict with public health principles. People frequently rank glamorous, high technology services, such as heart transplants, above far more effective and cost effective interventions, like child immunisation and family planning.'

Rather than attempting to involve the public at a strategic meso level in making trade-offs about which sectors or care groups should receive a higher priority, when information and understanding are absent, a better way of involving the public may be on a one-to-one level through a more equal partnership with doctors in making decisions about individual treatment (Hunter 1993a; Moore 1996). This latter notion is explored further in Chapter 6.

The remainder of this section reviews attempts to involve the public in rationing. The topic is perhaps the most divisive in the whole area of rationing. There are also many different approaches being tried to tap public opinion. Indeed, it is likely that the views expressed by members of the public will be as much a product of, or conditioned by, the methodology used as the knowledge base or views held by the individuals themself.

The methods for eliciting the public's views include surveys of public opinion, rapid appraisal at local level, health panels, focus groups and citizens' juries. All carry resource implications with techniques like citizens' juries being especially resource-intensive. Bowling (1996) reports that a number of local surveys of the priorities of the public and doctors have been conducted in the UK but no published nationally representative surveys of health-care priorities exist anywhere in the world. Until, that is, the survey she conducted to obtain the views on priorities for health services of a random sample of the British population. For Bowling, probably the most important shortcoming of the setting of public priorities is that priorities chosen by the public do not necessarily offer the most equitable solutions in relation to the founding principle of the NHS of equal treatment for equal need. Bowling's research confirmed the results of earlier surveys:

the public's priorities are not value free – they are most likely to prioritise treatments specifically for younger rather than older people and particularly life-saving treatments; [the research] also shows some public support (42 per cent) for people with self-inflicted conditions receiving lower priority for care, which raises ethical issues.

(Bowling 1996: 673)

As Bowling argues, if there is a conflict between the public's expressed values and the medical evidence on effectiveness or if prejudice against certain groups can be detected then there is a need for sound, unbiased information to be provided, coupled with effective public education. But these issues remain to be satisfactorily resolved – not just in the UK but in other countries too (see Chapter 5).

Using public ratings as the basis of health planning is fraught with ethical and logistical difficulties which merit further discussion (Bowling, Jacobson and Southgate 1993). Some of the key issues are as follows. If it is thought feasible and desirable to consult the public on health priorities, how can the public's voice (or voices) be heard most effectively? In particular, how can minority groups best be accessed? Is the unavoidable expense justified? How can the public be presented with information on health needs, outcomes and effectiveness in ways that do not oversimplify complex issues while giving them a knowledge base from which to express their views? How can conflicting views about health priorities, both between sub-groups of the population as well as between the public and health professionals (including the research community) be resolved?

Before the 1991 NHS changes most exercises in public consultation revolved around hospital closures – they were not primarily concerned, as is now increasingly the case, with the general canvassing of opinion about needs or priorities or with ranking procedures to establish those which should receive high priority and those which should not. Initial enthusiasm for consulting the public has, more recently, given way to much greater caution about how far health authorities should feel bound by the results of public consultation exercises they have launched. Few would subscribe to a pure notion of public sovereignty especially if there is an evident conflict between local public views and national policy priorities. Take the following example of seeking public views on how people in the community would rank AIDS sufferers against the claims of low-weight, premature babies. The example is taken verbatim from a transcript of *File on Four*, BBC Radio Four, 14 July 1992. This edition of the programme took rationing as its theme.

Person A: Not being bigoted or anything, I would feel that the young babies would be a priority because with the AIDS patients – not that it's necessarily their fault, nobody is ill of their own accord, or very rarely, but at least they've had some sort of life, whereas a premature baby or deformed child does not.
Person B: AIDS, I think, I'd let drop a little bit, and premature children, they've got a future.
Person C: I would say premature babies, depending on how the person got AIDS. If it was self-inflicted, tough, because apart from Arthur Ashe, who got that through a heart transplant or through a heart operation which isn't his fault, but other people, they get AIDS through their own morals or whatever, drugs, abuse, that sort of thing, then obviously I would prefer it to go to the premature babies, because that isn't their fault.

Views like this present a real challenge to health authorities. They must balance the differing views that they will gather not only from the public but from their own professional advisers and from the priority statements coming from government and elsewhere (see Figure 4.1). The example of AIDS illustrates how difficult it is to base decisions on the strength of public views alone. In the case of AIDS, central government has already made provision for AIDS sufferers a key priority. Yet, if the public's views are simply disregarded, what is the purpose of obtaining them in the first place, and what does it do to future relationships with the public who will surely begin to see the exercise as nothing other than a symbolic attempt to solicit their views? The role of health authorities as 'champions of the people' surely risks being perceived as cynically inspired? Even if it is the case that health authorities are engaged in a genuine exercise in public consultation it is vitally important that they are seen to be so engaged by the public themselves. As Bowling, Jacobson and Southgate (1993: 851) put it: before embarking on public consultation exercises, health authorities must ask themselves, and answer, one question: 'What will they do if they disagree with the results?'

In City and Hackney Health Authority, an approach to public consultation using questionnaires was tested in 1992 (Bowling, Jacobson and Southgate 1993). Respondents were asked to list 16 health services on a scale of priority ranging from essential to less important. In keeping with the results from other studies, the public prioritized life-saving technologies as high, as opposed to community services and services for people with mental illnesses which they prioritized as medium to

Figure 4.1 Balancing pressures
Source: Adapted from Ham, Honigsbaum and Thompson 1993: 9.

low, in contrast to all the samples of doctors. The public also prioritized infertility treatments, health education and family-planning as fairly low, as did the GPs and consultants, in contrast to the public health doctors who prioritized them as high. So the survey was telling the health authority that there were divergent views between the public and many professionals and that the public valued life-saving treatments at the expense of what they saw as peripheral services or less deserving causes.

It appeared that the majority of people emphasized quality of life rather than length of life in terms of treatments. Two-thirds of those consulted thought that people should not necessarily be kept alive when in pain or when dying anyway or when they have got a very poor quality of life. The results were also contradictory since many people had prioritized as very high those high-technology life-saving procedures that may or may not enhance the quality of life. But the survey revealed more than the fact that people could hold contradictory views. More important, it showed that medical questions are often so complex that altering the explanation of a procedure in the questionnaire produced a dramatic shift in the importance attached to it, to the extent that most estimations of what the respondents meant were meaningless. This evidence left the local managers in City and Hackney extremely wary about the value of public consultation. In the BBC Radio Four programme mentioned above, the Director of Public Health in City and Hackney is quoted as saying:

The wording of questions in this kind of research is always critical, and you can get the answers you want if you rig the questions. And in our pilot surveys, we found that rewording certain questions made a lot of difference to the answers. So, for example, most people in most of the community groups valued any interventions that were aimed at children very highly, in particular so-called life-saving services for premature babies. Intensive care services for premature babies were very highly valued when we first piloted this question. When we then amended the question to something along the lines of intensive care services for premature babies who are unlikely to survive this then received a much lower priority which suggests to my mind that if the public answering the questions had access to the same kind of information that I've got access to, knowing for example how effective family-planning services are, how effective immunization and breast-screening services are, I am sure that in my community we'd actually get a much better uptake of these services, as well as very high value for these services. I think we are asking the public very difficult questions in a vacuum which we in part are responsible for because we have not done enough homework and put enough effort into informing people about the background to these choices.

While a barrier to the democratization of decision-making is the lack of information provided to the public, this may not be easy to provide especially in an inner-city population where English is not the first language in a significant section of the community (Bowling, Jacobson and Southgate 1993).

If health authorities pursue a rather mindless or manipulative approach to public consultation of the type which some have indulged in then there is a risk of establishing a dictatorship of the uninformed. In support of the Director of Public Health from City and Hackney, Klein believes that some medical decisions are too complex even to ask the public for its opinion on them. Interviewed on the same radio programme he argued:

When you are designing surveys it is extraordinarily difficult to design questionnaires which actually mean anything. You can go out, grab people by the sleeve, and ask them 'Well, how would you rank the following procedures? Would you rather spend money on chiropody, would you rather spend it on tearing up the waiting lists and all the rest of it?' I don't think you're going to get answers to those questions which mean anything unless people have got an awful lot of context. I don't think you can provide them with that kind of context when you just send them questionnaires.

If you were to come up with a questionnaire asking me to rank my own priorities I would first want to know what we are doing at the moment, what are we spending our money on at present, what can we do with that money?

I would then go on to ask 'Well, what do you know about unmet need? In which areas can you give me a bit of evidence about inadequate services at the moment?' And I think it's only after a series of probing questions like that that I'd feel even remotely competent to rank priorities in the health service.

While valuable learning is taking place within health authorities about how best to have a meaningful dialogue with the public, problems remain about what you do with the different opinions collected. Of the many voices of the public, who should managers be listening to at any particular time? How can we be sure that all views have been captured from a population, large sections of which are unaccustomed to being consulted about anything, let alone life-and-death issues or complex matters of priority-setting?

It is concerns such as those described above which lead Doyal (1995) to oppose decisions arrived at simply because a majority has deemed it appropriate to deny health care to individuals or groups. In his view, 'democratic decisions can be both immoral and irrational' and can be 'distorted by secrecy, corruption and the influence of vested interests' (1995: 85). Therefore, even if the methodological problems in consulting the public can be overcome and cost is not a barrier, the bigger question remains: are community values the right ones to reflect in decision-making? They might, as Bowling, Jacobson and Southgate's 1993 study found, result in priorities which are contrary to the spirit of equity and equal access according to need (which is also Doyal's objection to public consultation exercises) which remain the founding principles of the NHS. Most of the discussion surrounding involvement of the public in priority-setting/rationing decisions has centred on technical concerns but more important are the ethical issues which have received rather less attention. The assumption has been that public involvement at this level is *a priori* welcome and a good thing. But is it?

The technique which probably goes furthest and deepest in terms of exploring issues, reviewing evidence and educating the public is the citizens' jury (Lenaghan 1997c). Though the idea is not new, having its origins in the USA and Germany, its introduction into the UK and the NHS has been through organizations like IPPR and the King's Fund. Its main distinguishing feature, in contrast to opinion polls, is that a jury tells you what the public thinks if individuals have a chance to be well informed about the topic and have time to exchange views and deliberate on it. Unlike focus groups or panels, a jury is not a resource for a health authority which may want to find out what the public feels. A jury is a channel for the voice of the community.

Citizens' juries go further than other mechanisms in conferring authority and status on the jurors as representatives of the community, acknowledging them as competent decision-makers. Juries do not confer executive power on jurors since their decisions are not binding. But jurors can call for additional evidence, examine expert witnesses, vary the questions suggested, and offer advice and recommendations to the commissioning authority.

IPPR has funded four pilot citizens' juries in conjunction with health authorities while the Local Government Management Board, in a parallel exercise, has put up funds to conduct a pilot with five local authorities. The pilot juries, in which the King's Fund is involved as evaluators, have been designed to test the methodology, to find out what the problems and pitfalls are, to pool experience and to develop a consensus about how a jury is run. One of the pilots – the first, held in conjunction with Cambridge and Huntingdon Health Authority in March 1996 – addressed three broad questions linked to the rationing debate. It was an issue of direct concern to this health authority which had been at the centre of national interest as a result of the Child B affair (see Chapter 1, Box 1.1). The questions addressed were: What is the NHS for? What criteria should guide decisions? Who should decide? To help shed light on the broader questions the jurors considered two practical examples: pacemakers and deviated nasal septums. They were asked whether a national body or individual local authorities should decide health-care priorities and were also asked to assess the value of public involvement in decision-making and of the citizens' jury model of involvement.

Selection for members of a jury should occur through market-research techniques in order to ensure a cross-section of the community. The optimal number of jurors is 12 but juries range in size from 10 to 24. Juries usually meet over four days. Jurors are paid for their time. A jury's conclusions are not binding on the commissioning authority but the expectation is that the authority should agree in advance to publish the fact that the jury is being held and the questions it is addressing, publish the jury's conclusions, respond within a set time, and offer an explanation for following or not following its recommendations. Juries do not come cheap: each one costs between £16 000 and £20 000.

Citizens' juries are not intended to supplant or pre-empt other forms of consultation or decision-making. Their purpose is to amplify and deepen the process of policy deliberation and decision-making. A number of lessons have emerged from the pilots conducted so far and these are listed in Box 4.7 (Coote 1996; Lenaghan 1996, 1997c).

A project on consulting the public in Somerset has been described by its principal consultant as a 'quick and dirty' version of the citizens' jury (Richardson 1996). The project, established and supported by Somerset Health Authority, was keen to build a consensus in the local community on resource allocation and values. It started in 1993 as a two-year project but is now a permanent mechanism. Eight health panels have been set up across the county each with 12 members on a rolling one-year membership basis to ensure constant new blood. It meets three times a year to discuss issues set by the authority. Panel members vote on the issues when discussion is complete. Detailed information on the subject is provided before discussions begin. There are no expert witnesses, only a well-briefed moderator. As at May 1996 eight events had been held at a cost of £35 000 to £40 000 per year. Richardson claims that the panels have made a real impact on the

Box 4.7 Lessons from citizens' juries pilots

- Full knowledge and consent of senior managers and others should be obtained at the outset.

- Preparation of timetable, evidence and witnesses is a complex and time-consuming process; human resources required should not be underestimated.

- Prior consultation with relevant interest groups, e.g. CHCs, is very helpful.

- Agreed rules of procedure must give priority to demonstrating the integrity and independence of juries.

- Question of openness remains unresolved: need to balance ensuring credibility in order to develop juries' legitimacy with avoiding any interference with their deliberations.

- Specific questions are easier for a jury to address than broader ones.

- Citizens' juries can be of two types: decision-making (deciding between options) and deliberative (considering more general questions and reaching a broad view about them).

- Technical adviser is needed to complement the independent moderator/facilitator.

- Sufficient time must be allowed for jurors to deliberate on their own.

- Separate male and female subgroups can overcome the tendency of men to dominate the discussion.

- Jurors gain in confidence over the course of a four-day session.

- Public enthusiasm for juries is tempered by deep cynicism about the possibility of them making a difference.

Source: Coote (1996).

health authority's decision-making process. The kinds of issues discussed include whether smokers should get a bypass operation, whether elderly people on waiting lists should get priority, and whether people should be allowed to have treatments outside the county.

It is probably too early in the history and development of these various mechanisms to engage more actively with local communities to say whether or not they are effective, are valued by both managers and public and, possibly most important, can be defended on cost-effective grounds. The answers to such questions will probably be forthcoming over the next few years. However, it is worth noting that there are many staunch defenders of citizens' juries and health panels, including those who were previously sceptical of their value. Reflecting on the nature of consultation and rationing as it operates in the NHS, Coote (1993: 40) observes that it:

can be an effective way of feeding the views of the public (as citizens or as customers) into decisions about rationing. How effective it is, from the public's point of view, depends on what questions are asked, by whom, of whom, by what means and on the basis of what information; on whether any *dialogue* takes place and, if so, with whom; on how the answers are processed and conclusions drawn, and on what action is taken as a result. All these decisions remain in the hands of those who consult – as in the decision whether or not to consult in the first place. At worst, it can be a highly manipulative process, benefiting no one but the consulting body. At best, it can be a route towards more open and appropriate decisions, more enlightened decision-making and a better-informed public. If the process is thorough it doesn't come cheap.

These points are all important. At a time when public cynicism about appointed, undemocratic bodies and about managers who are not account-able locally but who are the agents of government ministers is high, efforts to consult the public, however sophisticated technically, may be viewed with considerable suspicion and interpreted as gimmicks which are not to be taken seriously. This is why the point Coote makes about what action is taken, if any, as a result of consultation is so important. If the consultation exercise is seen to make no impact, however sound the reasons, it is likely to fuel the cynicism that may be present even if latent.

Exercises in consultation are an important part of participatory demo-cracy although how far they should inform priority-setting, given the moral objections noted above, is a major policy issue which has not been satisfactorily addressed. On their own, consultative exercises may afford insufficient safeguards against the abuse of authority which unelected and undemocratic bodies may be capable of perpetrating. As Doyal (1995: 85) cautions: 'Decisions which are supposedly representative of democratic wishes may not in fact be so.' They may be distorted by secrecy, bureaucratic processes or by organizational politics. On the other hand, authorities elected periodically would probably be insuffi-cient to ensure effective and ongoing accountability. What is required is a continuing dialogue with the electorate in which the public can both obtain and provide views while the authority is open to scrutiny, listens and (hopefully) responds. As Coote and Hunter (1996) put it, the ideal arrangement to ensure effective accountability is for active, par-ticipatory democracy to complement, validate and enrich representative democracy. But there is also scope for thinking afresh the whole local governance function and the nature of local government in health care. For instance, there is a body of opinion which argues strongly in favour of giving local government a major role by placing health commission-ing within its remit (Harrison *et al.* 1991; AMA 1993; Harrison and Hunter 1994; Clarke, Hunter and Wistow 1995, 1997; Cooper *et al.* 1995; Coote and Hunter 1996). According to Harrison and Hunter (1994), delegating to local government responsibility for purchasing health care would offer a number of important benefits to health policy. Only the first is relevant for the purpose of this discussion: namely, that it provides a solution (or at least a partial one) to the 'democratic deficit' problem whereby the 'new magistracy' of political appointees to health authorities would be replaced by elected members. This would provide democratic legitimacy for rationing decisions. The NHS suffers from a lack of openness, transparency and democratic accountability which the accountability and openness codes of practice do little to offset (Department of Health 1994; NHS Executive 1995).

This claim has not gone uncontested especially from those who are committed to, and benefit from, the present arrangement. Arguments against local democracy fall into two categories, both employed by NAHAT (1993), now the NHS confederation, and its Director, Philip Hunt (Hunt 1993). The first argument accuses local government of not really being democratic at all, but of being over-politicized and over-bureaucratized with members taking the important decisions and, as a consequence, a reduced role for managers. Harrison and Hunter (1994) challenge this view on the grounds that it is contradictory. The fact that members take decisions surely makes local government more, rather than less, democratic. Central government, which would otherwise continue to control health policy, can hardly be said to be democratic when the Executive effectively dominates the Legislature. At best, democracy consists of periodic general elections.

The second line of argument is that local government control would undermine the national character of the NHS by introducing local variance in the range of services provided. This is precisely the point of the local government option. It can be seen as both a strength and a weakness by its supporters and detractors respectively. A degree of national consistency in respect of the criteria to be adopted for rationing health care would be desirable. This could be provided for by, for example, prohibiting the use of purely social judgements (e.g. about lifestyle) in establishing entitlement to services or treatments, and by requiring local authorities to pursue equity of outcome in terms of survival and physical health as well as autonomy. Within these broad constraints, local authorities would be free to ration health care in a variety of ways. These could include establishing broader objectives within which waiting lists and clinical freedom would dispense rough justice. The details do not matter at this stage. What is important is to establish the principle of democratic control over decisions governing priorities in health care. Valuable though user involvement may be (and this is a highly contentious issue in itself), it is no substitute for effective accountability at the level of strategic planning. Elected agencies provide the essential legitimacy which no 'local voices' initiative can (or should) be expected to match. As was stated earlier, rather than seek to engage the public directly at a strategic, meso level about determining priorities or making choices, with all its attendant difficulties, it may be more productive to concentrate on the individual's relationship with their doctor or their contact with health-care services in order to equalize the power imbalance which is currently a feature of these relationships and contacts. This point is developed in the final chapter.

Conclusion

This has been a long and detailed chapter which has covered a great deal of ground. It seemed appropriate to contain the material within a single chapter since the topics covered are all closely related in practice even if they are often treated as discrete entities.

Repeated calls for a national approach to, or lead on, rationing have so far not been heeded. Indeed, the Conservative government is on record as having firmly rejected such a development on the grounds that it simply does not make sense when so much of health-care decision-making is context-specific and concerns individuals and must therefore be the responsibility of clinicians working at the local level (Secretary of State for Health 1996). A national approach need not mean only a rights-based approach to the availability of and access to health care. It could centre on establishing appropriate processes and procedures governing the delivery of health care, i.e. a system of procedural rather than substantive rights although in a diluted and faltering way the *Patient's Charter* can be seen as a step in this direction. But even here the Conservative government proved reluctant to assume responsibility for such a system of rights. A consequence has been the assertion that local practices vary unacceptably in a *national* health service.

With the focus quite clearly on local approaches to rationing, efforts at this level to improve both the knowledge base of decision-making and the influence over its outputs by the public need to be understood. There is also a tension inherent in these two approaches because while the technocratic approach emphasizes the importance of independent, objective, rigorous and scientific research to inform decision-making, the participatory approach puts the emphasis on the subjective, value-based nature of decisions. While there need not be a contradiction or conflict between these approaches, in practice there could be. If there is, then inevitably one or other approach will dominate – which is hardly in the spirit of regarding them as mutually reinforcing and complementary.

The review of current practice at local level in respect of rationing cautions us against expecting dramatic change or departures from the *status quo*. Evidence-based medicine and clinical effectiveness may be talked-up by ministers and researchers but if the past is anything to go by, as well as the present, then our expectations should remain modest. Indeed, recent research into how the NHS is responding to the clinical effectiveness/EBM agenda confirms this assessment of the state of policy (Walshe and Ham 1997). But even if EBM grips as intended and a culture of effectiveness begins to permeate the NHS, there will be a need to ensure that efforts to stimulate public involvement do not run counter to attempts to strengthen the knowledge base. Efforts to involve the public need to be thoroughly evaluated for their value and impact. They are not costless in terms of human and financial resources and time. Moreover, it remains unclear whether they owe more to gesture politics than to a genuine desire to shift the balance of power away from managers and practitioners.

What this review of developments in rationing health care in the UK at national and local levels shows most clearly is that all those engaged in the business of getting more for less from the NHS are desperately searching for solutions and best practices. A great deal of experimentation is evident although no one would claim yet to have found the optimal approach. In the midst of all this activity and search for a more rational approach to rationing, what can the experience of other countries teach us? The next chapter seeks to find out.

PART THREE

Health-Care Rationing: Lesson-learning and Future Prospects

CHAPTER 5

International approaches to rationing health care

Introduction

Earlier chapters have made passing reference to the experiences of other countries in the area of rationing health care. This chapter reviews the available evidence from a number of countries, each of which has sought to confront the rationing dilemma in a different way. There are essentially two approaches to rationing health care in evidence: a restricted list or basic basket of essential core services which are provided through the public system with the ability to top-up from private income, and the adoption of a framework or set of principles to give guidance in rationing decisions. While the former is much more prescriptive in character, the latter is much looser and open to flexible interpretation. To illustrate these various approaches, the experiences of the State of Oregon in the USA, New Zealand, The Netherlands and Sweden have been selected for scrutiny in this chapter.

The approaches to rationing adopted by other countries are often held up by critics of British practice, where there is a stoical refusal on the part of government to lead a public debate on the subject, as examples of what Britain could achieve if it wanted to. This claim rather exaggerates the achievements of others and assumes they have succeeded, or that there have been at the very least useful gains in policy terms, where Britain has failed but the evidence available offers little support for such a view. Even where attempts have been made to provoke public debate and get transparency into the processes of rationing, there continues to be a struggle over what precisely is to be rationed and whose responsibility it is to take the decision. In any event, it is never advisable to copy or mimic what may work in, or be appropriate for, one country in another with a very different culture, political system and health-care structure.

In what follows, it is not the intention to provide a comprehensive, detailed account of developments in Oregon, New Zealand, The Netherlands and Sweden. Reference is made to source material which will provide this. (A useful set of papers covering the countries considered below can be found in Maxwell (ed.) (1995)). Rather, the aim in this chapter is to focus on the central issues and features of the various country experiences as these relate to health-care rationing as described in earlier chapters in order to show the differences in approach and to discover what the potential may be for policy learning in a UK context where no national initiative has been forthcoming or is contemplated.

On the Oregon trail

We begin with Oregon in part because it is the best-documented attempt at explicit rationing (see Honigsbaum 1992) and because it has gone furthest in seeking to engage the public in an exercise whose primary objective was to rank interventions so that decisions could be taken about which to include in the public system and which to exclude. Oregon has been hailed as a triumph by those who see it as a brave attempt to confront the unthinkable in a responsible way. Others are dismissive of the exercise on the grounds that, at least in its particular US context, it is an attack on those social groups dependent on publicly funded health care while not affecting the affluent middle class in any way. They also question its methodological fairness and robustness.

The architect of the Oregon Health Plan, the Governor of Oregon, claims that the success of the Oregon experience lies in his and his colleagues' willingness to confront a difficult political issue: how much and what kinds of health care is society prepared to pay for and why (Kitzhaber and Kenny 1995). For Kitzhaber, it is necessary for every country to answer the question: what is covered? But he also maintains that rationing need not adversely affect health and claims that the Oregon experiment sought to challenge two assumptions: that health care is synonymous with health; and that all medical services are of equal value and effectiveness. For these reasons increased access to primary health care was a key objective of the initiative.

The origins of the Oregon experiment lay in the wish of the State legislature to extend the coverage of the public programme, Medicaid, to all poor people instead of to only 58 per cent of the poor deemed eligible according to the poverty level set by the federal government. In order to cover all poor people, it was decided to prepare a priority list covering the whole spectrum of care. The aim was to define a basic package of care which would apply to everyone, not only the poor. A commission of 11 members was established to create the list consisting of five doctors, a public health nurse, a social worker and four consumers of health care. The initial attempt to prepare a list relied solely on the use of QALYs (which were reviewed in Chapter 4). However, as Honigsbaum *et al.* (1995b) report, the QALY approach produced so many anomalies that the experiment nearly collapsed. Reliable data were not available for many procedures especially in the areas of cost and outcomes.

The commission then tried an approach which, according to Honigsbaum *et al.* (1995b: 13–14), combined a listing by category with condition-treatment pairs ranked within the category that most applied to them. The categories were ranked in priority order, using 13 values supplied by the public at community meetings held throughout the State. The public was not considered competent to rank the values, so they were listed only according to the frequency with which they were expressed. These were (in order):

1 prevention
2 quality of life
3 cost-effectiveness
4 ability to function
5 equity
6 effectiveness of treatment
7 number benefiting (from the treatment)
8 mental health and chemical dependency
9 personal choice
10 community compassion
11 impact on society
12 length of life
13 personal responsibility.

The commission used its own judgement to group these values into three classes:

• essential to basic health care
• valuable to society
• valuable to an individual needing the service.

Prevention and quality of life appeared under all three headings, while the number benefiting, impact on society and cost-effectiveness were the other three values located in the essential group. Personal responsibility was not included. Out of this process came 17 categories of health care. Life-saving treatments with full recovery were put at the top, followed by maternity care; treatments with little or no effect were put at the bottom.

Condition-treatment pairs were then put into their proper categories and listed in priority order. The commission's judgement was critical in assigning items to a higher or lower rank. As Honigsbaum *et al.* (1995b: 16) noted: 'Intuition and a concern for political realities had to be applied before the list could be completed.' The commission succeeded in reducing the number of condition-treatment pairs from 1680 (on the preliminary list) to 709 (sent to the Stae legislature). Funds were only available to cover the first 589 items which left 120 items excluded from Medicaid funding. As Honigsbaum *et al.* (1995b: 18) note: 'Among the excluded items were eight from the 366 in the original "essential" group, 51 from 275 in the [second] group and 68 from the [last] group. On the preliminary list, all the transplants had come near the bottom, but now 12 out of 19 were covered.'

The judgement of the commissioners was critical in the final rankings. Sixty items changed coverage with 30 moving above line 587 and 30 going below. There were several revisions to the initial list. It finally stood at 696 items with 565 funded. All references to quality of life were eliminated and medical effectiveness was used to rank services. Although an impressive list of public values was produced, the community meetings from which they emerged were not representative of the general public. 'About two-thirds of those who attended were workers employed in the health services' (Honigsbaum *et al.* 1995b: 20).

Public input to guide the ranking of health-care services was sought in three areas. First, public satisfaction with a variety of disability states was obtained from a random telephone survey of more than 1000 Oregonians. In the survey, respondents were asked to rate 26 disability states on a scale of 1 to 100 according to how happy/satisfied they would be with the disability. The results were collated into a weighting factor by level of disability and applied to the closest probable outcome in the cost-utility formula. Second, values placed on nine broad service categories were obtained from 46 public meetings held across the State. The participants were asked to assign each service category into one of three groups: essential, very important or important. The values that guided the groupings were then identified and discussed. From experience at the meetings, 13 fundamental values, including quality of life, prevention and cost-effectiveness, were distilled. These 13 values served as a guide in the construction of the priority list. Although more than 1000 Oregonians attended the public meetings, two-thirds were college graduates and fewer than 50 were recipients of Medicaid, that is, the public provision of care for poor people. As noted above, most of those attending the public meetings were also health care employees.

The third method of securing public input was linked to specific services. Views on these were solicited at seven public hearings. These meetings allowed special pleading by individuals and interest groups and the results of this consultation process were also fed into the databank to help shape the final ranking of priorities.

A worry about public involvement in Oregon is expressed by Dixon and Welch (1991). They point to the problems and drawbacks of engaging the public in establishing priorities and note that participants in open meetings may not be representative of the population at large and may include, as happened in Oregon, a disproportionate number of health-care employees. But it is not simply a matter of ensuring representative sampling. Certain sections of the population are more articulate and able to give voice to their preferences and wishes than others and able to do so through the medium of public meetings. Those sections of the population that for one reason or another are unable to articulate their concerns, especially in such a forum, may require the services of advocates to act as proxies.

Not surprisingly, the Oregon experiment has caused sharp divisions among academics, policy analysts, policy-makers and practitioners. There are those who consider it a courageous example of State leadership in a difficult area of public policy and those who have levelled all kinds of criticisms at the scheme, objecting to it on methodological, political and moral grounds. Klein (1992b: 1457), for instance, suggests that Oregon 'holds out a warning rather than offering a model for import into Britain: a warning that there are no ready made techniques for determining choices among competing priorities in health care'. If nothing else, Oregon's approach to rationing subjected the topic 'to the noisy debate it deserves' (Thorne 1992: 25). Criticisms of the Oregon plans have centred on two aspects: the technical problems of employing a cost-utility approach, and the process of involving the public in priority-setting and the ethics of doing so particularly in respect of seeking views on which treatments should be allowed and which not allowed. As we saw in Chapter 4, many observers and analysts of health policy have expressed unhappiness with the concept of rationing based only on cost-benefit data. It is argued that any rationing process ought to have ethical input as well. Worries were expressed, too, that the effectiveness data required by a formula approach were seriously inadequate and may always be so and cannot therefore be said to constitute a sustainable or sufficiently robust basis for making choices about which treatments to provide. Moreover, again as we saw in Chapter 4, there is the inevitable difficulty of making any formula sufficiently sensitive to individual patients.

The Oregon experiment has attracted considerable attention in the form of published books and articles and from those visiting policy-makers and managers who have been on the Oregon trail to see for themselves how explicit rationing has been made to work. Much of the external comment, especially that of a more reflective nature, has been critical of the Oregon Plan. For example, Garland (1992) has identified five themes of ethical concern which observers of the evolving arrangements in Oregon have raised. Some of these are peculiar to the American 'system' of health care and need not detain us here. But two of the concerns raised have a wider relevance. First, it is asserted that the Oregon Plan 'amounts to a futile tinkering with a fundamentally defective system' (Garland 1992: 54) and that what is required is wholesale reform aimed at rooting out wasteful practices. This line of argument echoes that which asserts that any form of explicit rationing is being negative and defeatist and a capitulation to those who believe there is no alternative. Indeed, the most frequently (and persuasively) voiced criticism of the Oregon Plan is that it will serve to distract attention from precisely such fundamental systemic reform of the health-care system. Although this is not an issue of immediate relevance in the UK, it could be if the NHS is progressively replaced by a fragmented, mixed public–private system that is poorly regulated. Typical of this way of thinking is Tartaglia's (1992: 148) comment on the US position: 'What is of concern, therefore, is the thought that instead of devoting our collective energies to providing the solutions to the problems that have been outlined, we are merely going to accept the concept that change is impossible and proceed to a rationing program in this country.'

It would indeed be ironic if the USA moved closer to the notion of comprehensive health care as a solution to Oregon-type initiatives while the UK, as a consequence of the downward pressure on public expenditure, put at risk the validity of the NHS as a comprehensive system and saw rationing as a means of trying to square the circle. Such an irony is unlikely ever to come to pass in such stark terms but certain dynamic forces in the respective health-care systems are resulting in the problem of rationing being considered in these terms.

Second, there is the technical difficulty of constructing a prioritized list of health services. Health-care services may be too complex to be prioritized with scientific validity and asking the public to give their opinion is hazardous because they are likely to feel differently about specific services in the abstract as opposed to when they actually need them. To be fair to the architects of the Oregon Plan, they were well aware of such dilemmas and sought to arrive at an acceptable, though possibly still imperfect, list that combined public values and expert opinion into a set of allocation priorities.

Defenders of, even enthusiasts for, the Oregon Plan make a virtue of the explicit approach to rationing which underpins it. According to Daniels (1992: 189–90): 'It disavows rationing hidden by the covert workings of a market or buried in the quiet, professional decision-making of providers – either at the bedside or in allocating resources within fixed hospital budgets.' This issue of openness, transparency and publicity divides commentators and analysts as well as those inside the health-care system and recipients of care. Whereas Daniels believes that justice requires publicity and public accountability, though not necessarily direct, participatory democracy, others take the opposite view. For example, and writing before Oregon attracted international attention for its activities in this area, Calabresi and Bobbitt (1978: 198) assert that what they term 'tragic choices' are best made away from public view in order to preserve important symbolic values such as the sanctity of life. In their view, it is doubtful if there could be an open society 'whose values were sufficiently consistent to obviate the possibility that scarcity would bring about tragic choices'. This point echoes that cited in Chapter 4 and put forward by Gormally (1996). A more pluralistic society is unlikely to reach consensus on the values that should apply in rationing decisions especially when needs, wants and rights become hopelessly confused and when there is a conflict between collectivist and consumerist notions of health-care provision.

Daniels (1992) is critical of the community meetings on the grounds that they were unable to do justice to the complexity of the subject. Discussions were too superficial to develop a clear picture of community values. Technical subjects may demand indirect representation rather than direct participation. A weakness, as well as a strength, of the Oregon experiment was the attempt made to combine community preferences about services with professional or expert preferences.

The Oregon experiment is notable for being the only example of policy prescription that has been implemented in practice (Klein 1996). Although it has not been imitated elsewhere, as mentioned above, its ideas continue to influence discussions and debate. Oregon conforms to rationing by exclusion: that is, the denial of certain forms of treatment. What appeals most about the Oregon experience to UK observers of health policy and the issue of rationing is the visibility of the process and the attempt, largely, though perhaps without foundation in the light of earlier comments, seen as successful, to give democratic legitimacy to decisions about rationing. However, it must be emphasized that the community which took part in the exercise was not representative but heavily biased towards those working in the health-care system. So, despite all the efforts to engage the community, the end result owed more to the experts and their values.

As Oregon demonstrates from its abandonment of rankings determined by the use of quality-of-life and cost-utility measures (which ranked appendectomy below tooth-capping because although the former's medical benefits were higher these were outweighed by the lower cost of the latter) and its only partially successful attempt to include community values, there is no 'right' or 'correct', and certainly no 'perfect', way to set health-care priorities. The experiences of other countries, which are considered in the remainder of the chapter, amply bear this out.

New Zealand: defining core services

The New Zealand health-care system and its reform implemented in 1993 closely resembles the experience of the British NHS although many commentators would argue that developments in New Zealand have been more radical, have gone further down the internal market route and have taken place with surprising speed (Malcolm and Barnett 1994; Salmond 1997). More recently, a new government has sought to move away from a market model with its emphasis on competition and restoring a collaborative public service ethos. According to Salmond's analysis of events, 'not even the National Government would claim that its health reforms have been an unqualified success' (1997: 90). As in the UK, the health-care reforms have remained controversial and generally unpopular. Hence the desire on the part of the new government to undertake a further round of major health sector changes. So, once again, New Zealand may be a little ahead of the UK.

While wishing to retain the principle of universal access to health care, the government, for economic and financial reasons, decided to restrict the range of services to an essential core progressively defined according to the benefits provided. To undertake this task, the National Advisory Committee on Core Health and Disability Services – Core Services Committee (CSC) in abbreviated form – was established in 1992. The notion of 'core services' has its origins in private enterprise whereby businesses seek to define their core business and 'stick to the knitting'. Its adoption in the public sector is entirely in keeping with the principles of new public management described in Chapter 3.

The intention was that the core would, according to the Health Minister, Simon Upton (Minister of Health 1990–93) be the acceptable level of health care to which everyone would have access. Yet within seven months of its appointment the CSC, which had been charged with the task of representing to government the community's views on which services should form the core, decided not to proceed with this work. This was a significant shift because an explicit definition of a core of services to which everyone would be entitled was a crucial component of the reforms. Such a core was to become the floor of the health service and was, in effect, a form of explicit rationing which would replace the system of informal rationing which operated on the basis of waiting lists and the denial of care.

The CSC did consult with the public through various means including public meetings, submissions, surveys and so on. The abandonment of the Committee's terms of reference after a mere seven months followed agreement by CSC members that they had been set an impossible task. A decision was taken to redirect their focus. The CSC, in its first report, concluded that 'there is very little merit in drawing up a detailed list of services in some sort of priority order' (Core Services Committee 1992: 63). Instead, the Committee took the view that all existing publicly funded services should be regarded as the core. In a crucial and fundamental shift in its terms of reference, the CSC was now concerned with modifying access to existing services rather than defining the core as had been expected.

In direct contrast to the Minister's claims that existing services were unfairly rationed, the Committee claimed the health and disability support services currently being provided 'are the product of decades of reasonably commonsense and principled decision-making. By and large, the current core reflects fairly accurately the values and priorities of several past generations of New Zealanders' (Core Services Committee 1992: 63).

In reaching this view the Committee claimed its decision not to adopt a limited list approach had public and professional support. Explicitly drawing parallels with Oregon, the CSC believed it could end up with a system that was more unfair than the one already in existence because individual circumstances would not be taken into account. The CSC did not feel at all comfortable with an approach to core services that did not take account of individuals' particular circumstances. The emphasis should not be on *which* services were to be publicly funded but rather on *whether* and *when* a service should be publicly funded. In restating the problem in these terms, the CSC approach is not so different from that adopted by the British Conservative government when it asserted that no treatments should be subject to a blanket exclusion from the NHS but that clinical decisions would be needed over the amount of treatment to provide and when to administer it (Secretary of State for Health 1996).

The CSC's first newsletter, *The Core Debater*, explained the decision not to define the core in the following terms (CSC 1994: 1):

One of the first things the committee did decide was that the core could not simply be a list of services, treatments or conditions that would or would not receive public funding. Very early on we decided that that approach just wouldn't work – it would be impossible to implement because it would either have to be so broad as to be meaningless, or so rigid as to be inflexible and unfair.

One reason for the CSC's opposition to defining core services was public and professional reaction to the notion of a list of core services. On the whole this was hostile. People were opposed to the development of a detailed list on the grounds that it was complex, time-consuming, costly and divisive. Some people argued in favour of a broad, ethical framework with widespread public input. Criteria similar to the public values found in Oregon (cost-utility, quality of life, prevention, numbers who would benefit) were suggested (Honigsbaum *et al.* 1995b).

In refocusing its remit, the CSC moved from the broader allocative decisions and concentrated instead on the allocation of services at the individual level (Finlayson 1996). The key consideration was to be the benefit of a particular service to a particular person at a particular time. Four questions formed a framework for deciding the circumstances in which services should be publicly funded:

- what are the benefits of a service?
- is it value for money?
- is it fair?
- is it consistent with the community's values and priorities?

Although the CSC believed it would be possible to establish priorities for publicly funded health and disability services, it acknowledged the strong risk of 'gaming' the system whereby professionals would creatively diagnose a patient's condition to ensure that the treatment would be publicly funded.

Finlayson (1996) maintains that much confusion surrounded the CSC's position once it had moved away from its original terms of reference to define a set of core services. As a consequence, she claims, covert rationing was preserved. Through its refocusing the CSC defined many people as not eligible for publicly funded services on clinical and social grounds. Gleisner and Paterson (1995: 8) have criticized the CSC's shift in focus: '[It] falls far short of clarifying an entitlement package; it is inadequate as a principle of justice, it provides no basis for choosing; it begs the question about values and none of the priorities carry a price tag.' Malcolm (1997) offers an alternative view maintaining that the CSC went out of its way to define priority-setting criteria which were as explicit as possible. Indeed, it is this very explanation which has attracted international attention.

Finlayson (1996) quotes a former Director General of Health, George Salmond, as saying that the CSC was given an impossible task and that defining an explicit core was not practical: '[I]nternational experience from Oregon and elsewhere suggests that explicit definition requires the making of explicit political value judgements which are controversial and difficult and which few politicians are either willing or able to make' (quoted in Finlayson 1996: 188). Salmond believed that the CSC should turn its attention to assessing new and existing technology from an efficiency perspective. Indeed, in a later commentary on the New Zealand health-sector reform experience, Salmond (1997) noted the useful work undertaken by the CSC in its new guise (see below) in developing evidence-based guidelines for the planning, purchasing and provision of services.

The CSC shifted its focus from being concerned with macro and meso level rationing (the first and second levels of Klein's categories noted in Chapter 2) to micro level rationing, i.e. the third and fourth categories. Because of its failure to define core services, the CSC was seen to sanction the covert rationing of health care through waiting lists and the denial of care. Doctors will continue to take responsibility for rationing services at the individual level, taking into account the CSC's guidelines for the services for which they have been developed (Finlayson 1996). But the *status quo* was not entirely endorsed. Nor would it continue wholly unchanged since the intention was to rationalize rationing through the encouragement of guidelines and by subjecting it to the disciplines of evidence-based medicine and clinical effectiveness criteria. One problem is that the CSC has failed to evaluate whether or not its guidelines have made any difference. It is likely that such efforts have made almost no difference (Malcolm 1997).

In recognition of its changed role the CSC was renamed in 1995 as the National Advisory Committee on Core Health and Disability Services – subsequently shortened to the National Health Committee. The Committee undertakes various community consultation exercises to elicit views about the values, like fairness and accessibility, that should drive the allocation of resources. Unlike some other initiatives elsewhere, the Committee has a continuing existence and can therefore assess priority-setting over time.

Although a core services approach to rationing has been abandoned, the Committee has begun to develop criteria to encourage the treatment of patients most in need first (Dixon and New 1997; Hadorn and Holmes 1997). This is held out as a possible model for the UK especially as there already exists a commitment to clinical effectiveness and evidence-based practice. Establishing priority criteria for specific services could be a logical next step in New Zealand with treatments known to be effective offered to the most needy patients first. The criteria combine clinical factors, like severity of illness and effectiveness of treatment, with social factors, such as the ability to work and to care for dependents. Higher-priority patients attract a higher-points score thus helping clinicians to decide who should be treated and when, and who should not. The approach has some similarities to that proposed by Doyal (1995) as an alternative to allowing the public to decide priorities. A form of triage based on immediacy and degree of need underpins Doyal's proposal. Patients are divided into three categories of priority: acute, urgent or elective, with treatment provided in this order in the same way for everyone. But the point about this approach, as Doyal acknowledges, is that it is already standard practice among health-care providers. However, social factors do not officially or formally form part of the calculus in terms of who gets treated when.

As Dixon and New caution, a number of important question arise in respect of the criteria being developed in New Zealand, notably about which clinical and social factors to include and how best to weight them. The level of funding dictates the number of points at which a patient can expect treatment so the approach cannot be seen as a way of putting pressure on government for an increase in public funding on health care.

Whatever else it demonstrates, the New Zealand experience holds no easy lessons for others seeking to adopt a similar approach. From its early abandonment of the attempt to define explicitly, and with public involvement, a list of priority core services, the Committee charged with the task shifted its focus from services to individuals and to how their access to appropriate services could be facilitated or not. It became more concerned with clinical effectiveness issues and less concerned with devising an explicit rationing scheme. The experience is of considerable interest in demonstrating how difficult it is to define a core package of services to which the public are entitled. The experience in The Netherlands, to which we now turn, is not dissimilar, notwithstanding important differences between the two approaches.

The Netherlands: defining key principles

The approach to rationing or making choices in The Netherlands has some parallels with both the Oregon and New Zealand experiences but also displays several distinctive features. The background to the Dutch approach lies in the proposals to reform the country's health-care system produced by the Dekker Committee in 1987. The central proposal was for a compulsory health-insurance scheme for everyone but based on a basic care package limited to 85 per cent of the health and social services previously provided. The government accepted the Dekker recommendations but expanded the basic care package to cover 95 per cent of existing services. A basic care package still has to be defined (Honigsbaum *et al.* 1995b). In order to define the basic package and achieve fairness in its operation the government set up the Committee on Choices in

Box 5.1   Criteria for rationing health care

- *The treatment must be necessary from the community point of view*: it does not make sense to incorporate unnecessary treatments in the health-benefits package.

- *The treatment must be demonstrably effective*: treatments whose effectiveness has not been demonstrated or are in doubt should not be incorporated.

- *The treatment must be efficient*: if there are two equally effective treatments, the cheaper one must be given preference.

- *The individual must assume responsibility*: if a treatment could reasonably be paid for by the patient, there is no reason to include it in the health-benefits package.

Source: Ministry of Welfare, Health and Cultural Affairs (1992).

Health Care. In 1990 the State Secretary for Welfare, Health and Cultural Affairs invited a cardiologist, Professor Dunning, to Chair the Committee. According to the minister, the main task of the Committee:

is to examine how to put limits on new medical technologies and how to deal with problems caused by scarcity of care, rationing of care, and the necessity of selection of patients for care.

The Committee should propose strategies to improve choices at different levels of health care. To accomplish this end, the Committee will have to analyse the problems that result from making choices at the national level (macro-level), at the institutional level (meso-level), and at the level of the individual caregiver (micro-level). The main outcome of these deliberations should be to stimulate a public discussion over the question, Must everything possible be done?

The State Secretary put three questions to the Committee to consider:

- why must we choose?
- what kinds of choices do we have?
- how should we make the choices?

The Committee reported some 14 months after being established (Ministry of Welfare, Health and Cultural Affairs 1992). Not surprisingly, its report did not attempt to give a single, definitive answer to these three questions but sought instead to set out guidelines for making fair choices. The report was regarded as a major contribution to public debate on choices in health care with a view to getting public support for future political decisions on health care. But although widely regarded as a useful exercise, it has not achieved its objective of winning public support for rationing decisions. Moreover, the report may have had more of an impact outside The Netherlands. It is certainly widely quoted and cited as an example of the kind of public discussion sought by many in the UK. But it has also come in for criticism, noted below,

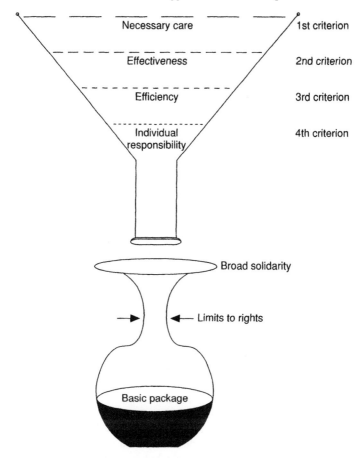

*Figure 5.1 **A system for setting priorities: The four sieves***
Source: Ministry of Welfare, Health and Cultural Affairs (1992).

about its limited value as a practical tool for those responsible for making rationing decisions.

The Committee took the view at the outset that choices in health care were both unavoidable and necessary. It opted for a community-oriented approach in which individual rights and professional autonomy are limited in the interests of equity and solidarity in health care. To meet this end, a number of strategies were put forward including restricting the rights of the insured, the use of waiting lists, the approval of medical technologies and the appropriate use of health care. Four criteria, listed in Box 5.1 (left), were proposed which should be met to justify the incorporation of a particular treatment in the health-benefits package of the health-insurance schemes.

As Figure 5.1 (above) shows, the four criteria are intended to serve as sieves so that each intervention should be evaluated against and satisfy each criteria. Everything that fails one of these need not be included in the basic package. So, the first sieve retains care which is unnecessary. The extent to which this is the case must be established by the community-oriented approach. The second sieve retains care with unconfirmed effectiveness or confirmed ineffectiveness. The third sieve retains care which is inefficient and less cost-effective. A treatment with low effectiveness and high cost would be excluded from the basic package. Finally, the fourth sieve retains care that may be left to individual responsibility. Limits to solidarity must not proceed on the basis of age, lifestyle or individual choice but are permissible when costs are high and the chance of an effect, i.e. capacity to benefit, very slight.

Using this framework, the Dunning Committee argued that dental care for adults, homeopathic medicines and IVF could be excluded from the care package. Beyond these interventions, the Committee argued that priorities should be set by assessing the effectiveness of health-care technologies and by devising explicit criteria for determining access to waiting lists and from waiting lists into hospital. The health-care professions were called on to take the lead in drawing-up guidelines for the provision of services. The key to further progress is seen to lie in influencing doctors' decisions in order to promote more effective clinical practice – a position not so different from the UK stance about evidence-based medicine and clinical effectiveness initiatives.

The Dunning Committee proposed that the Health Insurance Council should be charged with the task of identifying a number of categories of diagnosis/treatment combinations based on the nature and severity of the diagnosed condition and the nature, length and effect of the treatment. These categories would then be ordered according to the priorities in the community-oriented approach described by the Committee. What will finally be defined as necessary care will be determined not according to some technical formula but by political considerations. Political acceptability will therefore be the crucial test.

The Committee also challenged the notion of professional autonomy and sought a revised conception of it based on improved accountability. As it put it:

The individual professional will have to be accountable not only to the professional association, but also to the others involved. The community-oriented approach has thus a clear and direct consequence for the autonomy of the individual professional, whose expertise is not diminished, but whose actions must be accountable to third parties.
(Ministry of Welfare, Health and Cultural Affairs 1992: 119)

The Dunning Committee's criteria can be used to determine whether services should be included in the basic package of services to be offered. But they do not provide an answer to the question of how much health care should be provided. The four criteria are far from easy to employ in practical decision-making and it is likely there will be much discussion and potential for conflict among key stakeholders. Perhaps it is not surprising therefore that the impact of the Dunning Committee's proposals have been limited (WHO 1996; van der Made and Maarse 1997). Ministers have been reluctant to implement the recommendations although it seems that the present minister is more enthusiastic about them. She has announced her intention of using the four criteria for an assessment of all health-care benefits included in both compulsory health-insurance schemes. A consequence of any reductions in the coverage of these schemes is that those covered by compulsory insurance will opt for supplementary private health insurance. 'Amenity care' is to be transferred to supplementary health insurance. The government also intends to transfer to this element of the scheme any service item which cannot satisfy the four criteria of necessity, effectiveness, efficiency and collective responsibility (see Box 5.1) (Schut 1996). Dental care for adults and parts of physiotherapy services have already been shifted to this category as a result of applying these criteria. The government claims that dental costs are low enough to be left to individual responsibility (the fourth criterion) and the effectiveness of some physiotherapy treatments is not proven (the second criterion). Critics of these transfers to supplementary insurance assert that the government is motivated by a desire to reduce the share of collective expenditure on health care rather than a careful application of the four criteria. However, after intense political and public opposition, the decision to exclude dental care has been reversed (Van der Grinten 1997).

The Committee's hierarchy of priority in respect of the three perspectives – community, medical professional and individual – has been criticized for not being coherent (Harrison and Hunter 1994: 58):

The medical professional perspective is, in fact, the narrowest of the three and is therefore unlikely to include anything not covered by the broader community perspective. The implication of the hierarchy as proposed is simply that the doctor can only offer services available on the basic insurance scheme, and that the patient can only choose between services offered by the doctor.

It is also stated, as noted above, that care should not be of a kind that would more appropriately be left to individual responsibility. The significance of this last criterion is rather unclear since it is explicitly stated that such factors as age and unhealthy lifestyle are not to be employed as rationing criteria or constitute grounds for denying treatment. Smokers would have the same right to heart operations as non-smokers. Although the Committee was of the opinion that there is a moral obligation on individuals to protect their own health, it should not result in a reduction of solidarity in the basic package. 'Unhealthy or risky behaviour should be discouraged, but healthy behaviour cannot be imposed' (Harrison and Hunter 1994: 64). The Committee adopted the principle that everyone should have access to health care when it is needed, regardless of the reason.

While The Netherlands has gone furthest of perhaps any country in seeking to produce a national framework to guide the making of choices, it is not devoid of criticism. Nor has the framework so far impacted dramatically on practice. There is no national framework as such despite the plethora of reports (of which Dunnings' is the best known) and much division and effort at a policy level. The process is essentially evolutionary rather than systematic and planned (Van der Grinten 1996). But what is particularly interesting about the Dutch experience is the difficulty the Dunning Committee had in applying its four criteria to whether or not services, or parts of them, should be in or out of the basic benefits package (Van de Ven 1995). The reason for this is that the effectiveness of care has to be considered in relation both to the presenting condition and the condition of the patient. Clinicians are critical in such decisions and it is therefore their practices and modes of operating which demand attention if there is to be appropriate use and delivery of care. The current Minister of Health is a staunch support of evidence-based medicine and appropriate clinical behaviour in the use of resources. But she recognises the high potential cost of focusing on the existing basket of services where the room for manoeuvre is limited, and is focusing instead on new services and technologies. The Dunning report has therefore had only a limited impact in this respect.

If there is a common theme emerging from the experiences of different countries then it centres on the use of evidence in practice and the effectiveness of care, i.e. the micro level. The Swedish approach marks something of a departure in that it is principally concerned with ethical principles at a macro level, or with establishing what has been termed an 'ethical platform', and the extent to which it is possible to reach common agreement on them. The case of Sweden is the final example in our selected global tour of rationing practices.

Sweden: principles and priorities

Although the Swedish health-care system differs from the British NHS in a number of important respects, there is more commonality between them in terms of philosophy and approach than exists in most other European countries. Sweden operates what is famously known as the Welfare State 'without limits'. To admit that rationing is an issue at all in such a system is a highly sensitive, intensely political issue. Hardly surprising therefore that concern over priority-setting is of fairly recent origin in Sweden. The government appointed a Priorities Commission in 1992 which reported in 1995 (Swedish Parliamentary Priorities Commission 1995). The Commission was established to consider the responsibilities, demarcation and role of health care services in the Welfare State, to highlight the fundamental ethical principles which can furnish guidance and form a basis for open public discussion, and recommend guidelines for priority-setting in health services. The government took the view that an increased public awareness and greater understanding of the complex issues surrounding health care would be beneficial in themselves and possibly part of the solution (Calltorp 1995).

As part of its task, the Commission reviewed various attempts to set priorities such as those in Oregon, New Zealand, The Netherlands and Norway. As McKee and Figueras (1996: 692) report, it found each wanting in crucial aspects but 'usually their superficial exploration of ethical issues or their tendency to gloss over methodological problems in measuring efficiency'. Following a wide consultation process involving key stakeholders both inside and outside the health-care system, the Commission established three ethical principles in rank order, i.e. the last is given relatively low priority:

- *human dignity*: all individuals regardless of age and lifestyle are of equal value and none should receive preference in care because of personal characteristics or status in the community (patients paying privately could have improved amenities but not a higher standard of care)
- *need and solidarity*: resources should go to those who need them most, particularly to vulnerable groups like the mentally ill
- *cost-efficiency*: the most cost-effective care should be provided but comparisons of interventions are possible only for the same diseases – the Commission rejects the efficiency principle for deciding on priorities between programmes because fair comparison of the effects is impossible; it should only apply when comparing methods for treating the same illness.

Under the Swedish approach, micro level priority-setting would remain the responsibility of doctors. The Commission also ruled out a basic package of care, maintaining that most medical care activities should be jointly and equitably funded (Honigsbaum *et al.* 1995b).

Priority-setting in Sweden is advancing cautiously on the basis of experience acquired from local developments in the county councils and from other countries. It has eschewed a narrow technocratic approach based on establishing a core service in favour of one which is governed by an ethical framework to guide decision-making on the use of resources. A non-prescriptive approach has been adopted for guidelines or financial incentives. It is acknowledged that there are no easy solutions.

The Commission sought to establish clinical and administrative priorities, recognizing that these might differ. In fact the differences proved not to be so great. The priorities were seen as belonging to one of five categories, listed in rank order (Calltorp 1995):

- treatment of life-threatening acute diseases and those which, if left untreated, will lead to permanent disability or premature death; treatment of severe chronic diseases; palliative terminal care; care of people with reduced autonomy

- prevention shown to be of benefit; rehabilitation and so on as defined in the Health and Medical Services Act
- treatment of less severe acute and chronic diseases
- borderline cases
- care for reasons other than disease or injury.

This list was intended to guide decision-makers and to stimulate discussions at all levels within the health-care system.

Unlike the Dutch approach, advocated by the Dunning Committee, the Swedish Commission did not make specific proposals for excluding services. In contrast, the Swedish approach starts from the recognition that there is no simple method of setting priorities and that priority-setting can only be carried out through a process of informed discussion utilizing a framework of the type produced by the Priorities Commission. Its importance lies in its symbolic value and the need for what is seen to be realism in Sweden's model of welfare (Calltorp 1995). It now faces the same problems as virtually all other health-care systems. In these circumstances, governments can help by providing information to inform decision-making but there is no magic formula which can replace what in the end are choices based on values and judgement. Most of these can only be made at the level of clinical decision-making about individual patients and are not candidates for solution at a higher political level. McKee and Figueras (1996) commend the Swedish approach to those in the UK calling on government to give a lead in rationing. Its appeal for them lies in its insistence that setting priorities is fundamentally an ethical issue requiring familiarity with theories of social justice and the need to state where a health-care system stands in relation to them. Once again, the desire to make rationing more rational is perceived as the overriding concern. There can be no room for *ad hoc* decisions and fudging the issue.

International experience: what can be learned?

The experiences of several other countries could have been included in the above selection of country profiles on rationing and priority-setting. But they would have reinforced the points made and issues already covered rather than add anything substantively new or distinctive to the discussion. What the experience of other countries all too clearly shows is that perhaps the UK is unusual in resisting the route they have chosen in at least having a national debate on the matter and attempting, as in Sweden's case, to begin to put in place a framework of ethical principles in order to structure the discussion and possibly provide guidance, for the most part of a fairly general nature, to decision-makers at macro, meso and micro levels.

Yet it is also reasonable to pose the question: so what if Britain is different and has chosen, as governments clearly have to date, to adopt a different approach? Does it matter? Has decision-making been any the poorer? Would priorities have been any different? It is one thing to have lofty grand principles and frameworks all made explicit and in the public domain, the real difficulty, as the experience of other countries demonstrates only too clearly, comes in translating these into practice and operationalizing them in respect of individual patients. This is a key concern in all the countries which have ventured down this path and to which, as the Swedes have found, there is no magic solution.

Moreover, on closer inspection and contrary to what is commonly alleged, the British NHS is not devoid of all principles and guidance. There is much in common already with the Swedish approach, albeit the UK's position is possibly more cautious and non-prescriptive. Nevertheless, there is an emphasis on the founding principles of the NHS, restated and reaffirmed in a Conservative government White Paper (Secretary of State for Health 1996), and on the importance of evidence-based medicine and clinical effectiveness (NHS Executive 1996). The outpourings from the NHS Executive and academic centres engaged in this work are ample testimony to the importance attached to, and significant investment in, these activities. There is also the health strategy, *The Health of the Nation* (Secretary of State for Health 1992) in England, and its counterparts elsewhere in the UK, which explicitly identifies key areas meriting priority in respect of health care, including preventive and rehabilitative as well as acute interventions. From the experience of other countries, it is not very obvious or self-evident what more can usefully be done unless the intention is to go for a crude, imposed top–down system of rationing based on core services, a basic package or a restricted list of procedures. Yet, as we have seen, to attempt to follow this course of action would be likely to carry a heavy political cost and, in the end, prove unworkable. Take as an example the Dunning Committee's proposal that IVF be excluded from the basic package on the grounds that childlessness does not interfere with normal social functioning. This may be challenged on the grounds that for some people childlessness is a social dysfunction (Harrison and Hunter 1994; New and Le Grand 1996).

It seems, then, that when all the various initiatives and commission reports on rationing are studied the experience of other countries is not so dissimilar to that of the UK. As Klein, Day and Redmayne (1996: 118) conclude:

setting priorities or devising criteria for rationing turns out to be a peculiarly intractable endeavour, where practice lags behind rhetoric. There appears to be no generally acceptable technical fix, such as cost-benefit analysis, for resolving the dilemma encountered. Similarly, there is nothing like a universal model: the various countries . . . are unanimous only in rejecting the Oregon prototype.

What the evidence from other countries clearly demonstrates, including evidence from countries not considered here like Spain and Germany (see Lenaghan (ed.) 1997b), is that the adoption of a guaranteed entitlement to health care is extremely difficult to operationalize. Moreover, the attempt invariably leads to inequity and the creation of a dual standard in health care. Interestingly, all the contributors to an international conference in 1995 on choices in health care organized by the Institute for Public Policy Research rejected the idea of a guaranteed entitlement to health care on the grounds that it was simply not feasible in practice. As Del Vecchio (1997) warned, explicitly defining priorities and attempting to enshrine them in a set of substantive rights can create social and political conflicts. This is a likely outcome in societies 'where technical rationality (as opposed to social and political rationality) is not fully accepted as a good means of defining priorities' (Del Vecchio 1997: 171).

Such concerns may explain the conclusion reached by WHO in its review of health-care reform issues, including priority-setting, in Western Europe. Despite various initiatives to examine priority-setting on a more systematic and explicit basis, 'overall, there has not been any substantial reductions in the coverage or package of benefits offered by their statutory systems' (WHO 1996: 106). The appeal of the Swedish approach is that it eschews a prescriptive and narrow mechanistic approach in favour of setting out ethical principles to guide decision-makers.

International experience is still evolving and, to a large extent, remains in its infancy. But on the evidence available so far, it provides no model or template to determine practice in the UK or anywhere else for that matter. As the WHO (1996: 110) review asserts, 'Priority-setting is inherently complex and is not amenable to a quick fix.' But some patterns and possible lessons can be discerned. A key distinction is to be made between rationing services by exclusion on the one hand and rationing by guidelines and protocols on the other. Oregon is an example of the former, while New Zealand, which started off down the Oregon road, quickly came to the conclusion that it was not possible and switched to a focus on effectiveness and on producing guidelines for clinical services. The Netherlands has adopted a mix of the two approaches but with only limited success so far because of the political pain of excluding services outright and opting for a basic package of core services. Whatever approach is adopted, it is acknowledged that an exclusive reliance on technical fixes is not acceptable or appropriate. Involving the public in the process of priority-setting is therefore regarded as vital and is a feature of all the countries studied. Methodologies for achieving this are at various stages of development, as they are in the UK (see Chapter 4). Again, it is not clear to what extent the public (whatever is meant by this term which embraces a plurality of different values and interests) is to be genuinely involved in real debate as opposed to playing a symbolic function in terms of legitimizing decisions or principles which will be determined by political and professional élites. The various moves to embrace the public appear to be a combination of both. It remains to be seen which perspective, if either, will triumph.

But there is a paradox which this review of international experience in the sphere of rationing has brought to the surface. On the one hand, the UK stands accused of complacency and of not taking rationing seriously with central government nonchalantly standing aside and refusing to give a lead on the necessary hard choices. On the other hand, in those areas where countries see the most potential for a more rational approach to rationing – clinical effectiveness and public involvement – the UK is either a leader or certainly an impressive performer. No other country has such a developed, nationally-driven R&D strategy, which in the UK underpins the evidence-based medicine (EBM) movement, and few countries can point to the variety of initiatives and experiments evident in the UK in respect of public involvement. As Chapter 4 concluded, it would be quite misleading to overstate the potential of either EBM or mechanisms for involving the public in priority-setting as far as finding solutions to the rationing dilemma is concerned. But the point about such ventures for present purposes is that they give the lie to the view that the UK is doing nothing when it comes to confronting making choices in health care. The evidence, especially when set alongside what is happening elsewhere, shows this not to be the case.

And this brings us to the final lesson from this selective review of international experience. As WHO (1996: 112) acknowledges, 'Each country needs to find its own solution to the priority-setting dilemma, reflecting its own starting point, levels of expenditure and expectations.' As this chapter has sought to demonstrate, a number of options and approaches are available which need to be constantly revisited in keeping with the dynamic, ever-shifting nature of health-care systems and services. But if no ideal or preferred model or template exists, then what, if anything, is to be done about the dilemma of rationing health care in the UK? Do we simply give up the search for a solution, however desperate the apparent need for one? Do we opt for a less than perfect one in the knowledge that none exists and in the belief that it is at least an improvement on the *status quo*? Or do we broadly maintain the *status quo* with some marginal adjustments? These questions are the subject of the next and final chapter.

CHAPTER 6

Issues and prospects

Introduction

Throughout this book, a single theme has dominated: the extent to which health-care rationing should remain implicit or become more explicit in recognition of the fact that not everything that can be done in medicine, even if it is of proven effectiveness (and it is a big 'if'), can be done. Indeed, the advocates of explicit rationing, or rational rationing, would argue that it is a dishonest pretence to perpetuate the myth, which they believe implicit rationing does, that all needs can be met and that it is not necessary to state explicitly, and be transparent about, the rules of the game so that all the stakeholders in health-care decision-making, especially the public, know precisely where they stand. Some commentators and practitioners subscribe to the notion of a core-service approach or restricted list or menu which seeks to establish a guaranteed entitlement to health care. Treatments not included in the package are either foregone or paid for privately.

A less hard-nosed approach opts for a set of guidelines or a framework of principles to govern decision-making and provide a reference point for a consideration of the complex ethical issues involved in priority-setting. Sometimes the language of rights is used to frame the debate and to provide a possible solution. These can be substantive or procedural and, if the former, parallel rationing by exclusion (i.e. the core-service approach). As Lenaghan (1997d: 193) defines rights, 'Substantive rights are specific and individually enforceable rights to actual resources, whereas procedural rights guarantee an individual access to fair and accountable decision-making processes.' For the truly hard-nosed rational rationers, nothing less than a system of substantive rights will suffice. Anything that falls short of establishing 'socially agreed criteria that determine access to limited NHS care' will be dismissed as 'inconclusive and diffuse' (Maynard 1996: 1499). This view is echoed by Doyal (1997) who also subscribes to the view that rationing should be made explicit at all levels. Not even to make the attempt to understand the criteria governing the allocation of resources and the rationing of these is a mark of defeatism and pessimism. Alongside all these facets of an explicit approach is the issue of how to engage the public in a debate about priority-setting and whether this is best done through the representative democratic process, through direct participatory methods, many of which, like citizens' juries, are still being tested, or a combination of the two.

It is the purpose of this chapter to pull together some of the key themes which have featured in preceding chapters and to offer a critical appraisal of these in the form of policy options. My preference for an approach to rationing that is based essentially on implicit rationing is then examined and offered as a possible way forward.

Policy options

In tackling the rationing problem there are a number of options available to policy-makers. These were introduced, and commented on briefly, in Chapter 2. They are revisited here in the context of the ground covered in Chapters 3 to 5, i.e. is there anything that can be learned from the developments described in these, and of the attempt in this final chapter to consider prospects for the future. The options to be considered differ from the earlier list with the addition of a separate heading on effectiveness to capture the developments in clinical effectiveness and EBM. The options are as follows:

- increased expenditure on the NHS
- greater efficiency and value for money
- greater cost-effectiveness through evidence-based medicine and clinical effectiveness
- voluntary restraint
- explicit rationing
- (masterly) inactivity.

A further option, which I prefer, and has not yet been considered in any detail though it was introduced in Chapter 1, is

- muddling through elegantly.

Each of these options is examined in turn. As mentioned, previous chapters have, to a greater or lesser degree, already touched on some of them. In this final chapter, the strands of the various arguments are brought together in an endeavour to chart a way forward which appears both sensible and politically realistic and sustainable while avoiding the naïvety and simplistic approach of those advocating either a menu-driven approach to health care or simply an open public debate on the issue of rationing with a view to getting agreement or broad social consensus to a framework of principles which might provide guidance to decision-makers. In reviewing in turn the various arguments and policy options listed above, the explicit versus implicit debate will be addressed and the pitfalls of explicit rationing considered.

Increased expenditure on the NHS

Many opponents of the notion of an open public debate on rationing such as Mullen (1995) and Best (1997) regard it as a move born out of despair. They believe it would be a more productive exercise to have a debate about the overall level of investment in the NHS since, as Best (1997: 13) reminds us, 'the UK spends less on health care than almost all other Western developed countries. Yet the rationers assume the hard choices about which services the NHS should provide need to be made against the backdrop of this low level of overall investment.' If, argues Best, the government were to devote another 1 per cent of GNP to the NHS this would not remove the need for choices but they would be different ones. And yet there is no public discussion of this way of viewing the problem. As Best asks: 'Why should the rationing take place *before* – or as an alternative to – the debate that determines the quantum of resources to be rationed?'

In similar vein, Mullen (1995) and Hunter (1993a) believe that a focus on explicit rationing could divert attention from a basic under-funding of provision. Indeed, Hunter (1993a: 24) goes further and fears that explicit rationing 'could blunt arguments for devoting additional resources to health care'. Mullen (1995: 25) suggests that whether the resources devoted to the NHS are insufficient to meet need and/or demand 'appears to be a matter of choice, not objective necessity'. She continues: 'Given that the NHS is already relatively efficient, the main focus would thus be on the overall level of resources allocated to the NHS, with a secondary focus on eliminating treatments proven to be, on balance, harmful.' But it is the 'climate of defeatism' (Mullen 1995: 26) created by calls for explicit rationing which is regarded as most counter-productive because it detracts from a wider debate about what sort of health service is wanted and required. The two issues are not unconnected for, as Best (1997) warns:

if explicit rationing is introduced at such a low level of investment, it will invariably undermine the principle of a publicly-funded NHS ... Clearly, the lower the level of expenditure on health care, the longer the list of treatments that will be excluded through rationing.

It is certainly true that some of the advocates of explicit rationing favour exactly such an outcome although they conceal their preferred outcome in language about clinical effectiveness and evidence-based medicine and the seeming inevitability of opportunity cost in a context where the provision of extra resources is extremely unlikely. For instance, the Healthcare 2000 group acknowledged the widespread perception among the public that the NHS is underfunded and cited evidence that people would be prepared to pay more for an improved service. It concurs with those who assert that when compared with other countries the UK spends below average on health care. But it goes on to note that the level of public expenditure on health in the UK is close to the international average and concludes that the main difference between the UK and other comparable countries is not in the levels of *public* funding (which are comparable) but in the levels of *private* funding. The reader is expected to infer from this that any additional resources to be forthcoming for health ought to come from private sources. In case any reader is slow to grasp this message, the Healthcare 2000 (1995: 39) report disposes of the case for increased public spending on health in a single sentence: 'It is unlikely that sufficient additional revenue will be raised by increased taxes, although public pressure and changing government priorities could result in bringing UK expenditure on health nearer to the OECD average.' But the authors of the report admit that there is no conclusive evidence that the NHS is underfunded (see also Dixon, Harrison and New 1997). Nevertheless, it does not prevent them stating that while remaining wedded to general taxation as the principal source of funding health care, it is not possible to expect the 'continuing gap between resources and demand to be closed through increased tax funding alone' (p. 9). Therefore a combination of strategies will be required which will 'include a clearer definition of what services will be provided free at the point of use and raising the proportion of health-care funding provided by individuals through options such as user charges and/or patient co-payments' (Healthcare 2000 1995: 9).

The Conservative government's response to this line of argument was that it remained resolutely committed to a tax-based NHS and believed the pressures on public funding were manageable. It took the view that not all the pressures on the NHS were ones which need entail cost-inflation. Some can be expected to free-up resources to redirect elsewhere. It also points out that the NHS has had to confront such pressures for all of its life citing the Guillebaud report from 1956 on *The Cost of the NHS* (Ministry of Health 1956). At the time it commented that 'The advance of medical knowledge continually places new demands on the Service, and the standards expected by the public also continue to rise.'

The Conservative government obtained broad endorsement for its position from the House of Commons Health Committee. In its report on priority-setting in the NHS it argued for a balanced view to be taken of cost pressures (House of Commons Health Committee 1995a). Mitigating forces are at work and medicine is a dynamic activity subject to constant change. For instance, improved knowledge of the causes of ill-health offers the opportunity to prevent, or slow the onset of, many previously unavoidable illnesses through health education and other initiatives. The Committee argues for a sustainable approach to the public's health since this would do much to ease the pressure on the NHS. Effective advocacy of public health issues must be a priority.

Hardly surprisingly, then, that the argument about underfunding and whether or not this is a problem for the NHS remains unresolved even though it is paraded at regular intervals. Certainly, rationing is no less a problem in countries like The Netherlands and Sweden which spend a higher proportion of their GDP on health care. But to conclude from this that there might not be benefits from increasing NHS spending would be unreasonable. As noted above, although additional investment would not eliminate the pressures on the NHS and the choices to be made it would significantly alter their nature and impact. However, additional investment could prove to be a short-term palliative diverting attention away from tackling inefficiences within the NHS.

Greater efficiency

The Conservative government remained convinced that year-on-year cost improvements in the region of 3 per cent per annum remained achievable although the view on the frontline is that major inefficiencies in non-clinical areas have probably now been successfully addressed. Future gains are likely to be marginal with major advances being achieved by looking much more critically at clinical effectiveness and evidence-based medicine. For instance, Roberts *et al.* (1995: 15) advance the notion that health-care rationing is 'highly premature' when 'the scale of inefficiency is well outside what might be accepted as an inevitable component of any large organisation'. Roberts and his colleagues put a figure of 20 per cent on the scale of inefficiency which, they state, can be backed up by data. Examples given of known inefficiencies include eliminating waste in acute bed days, unnecessary X-ray examinations and subsidies for social care from clinical resources. Many of the supporting data come from various Audit Commission studies, including those on day-case surgery and other clinical areas. For Roberts and his colleagues, the problem is not insufficient funds 'but poor management, which is failing to direct money where it is needed most'. This argument is supported by Light who urges that 'our goal should be to minimize the need to ration by eliminating ways that entrenched institutional, political, and professional interests lock in waste not to figure out how to ration fairly in the context of a segmented, unintegrated system with wasted resources. This is the real ethics of rationing' (Light 1997: 112).

As it happens, even management, which experienced significant growth and expansion following the 1991 NHS changes, has found itself vulnerable to cost-cutting exercises and downward pressure which has yet to run its course. But there is a paradox at work here: on the one hand, the government is anxious to streamline management and reduce the transaction costs associated with its predecessor's reforms. On the other hand, changes occurring in the area of primary care and other tasks such as clinical effectiveness seem likely to lend to growing pressure for additional investment in management and other types of infrastructure strengthening. Moreover, the move to primary care could reinforce the fragmentation that has become a more prominent feature of the NHS since 1991 with the arrival of the purchaser–provider separation and GP fundholding. It is also the case that the capacity of health authorities to deliver on the agenda set for them by ministers is proving problematic. A review of the functions, roles and costs of health authorities reported that health authorities 'are very constrained on resources to support important areas of work. Some, particularly low cost Authorities, are vulnerable on key objectives, *such as public involvement and clinical effectiveness*' (Griffiths 1996: para. 1.3, 3, emphasis added). These are precisely the areas which the government has sought to develop and stress the importance of in the context of priority-setting and rationing. The unequivocal message from Griffiths' report is that if health authorities are to deliver on a large and growing agenda, and to improve the efficiency and effectiveness of health care, then the 'current insufficient management capacity' needs to be tackled (Griffiths 1996: para. 1.4.9, 4).

There are implications in all this for the future of rationing at local level. Without effective management, which is probably a separate though not wholly unconnected issue from the number of managers, calls for rationing will surely grow and the efficiencies to be won will simply not be realized. In such circumstances, the future does not auger well for evidence-based medicine.

Greater cost-effectiveness through EBM

It is argued that major significant savings could come from challenging not only the effectiveness but the cost-effectiveness of medical care (Maynard 1996). However, as Chapter 4 tried to show, there are un-likely to be any quick wins in this highly complicated area. Even where the knowledge base is reasonably robust, it is unlikely to be possible to remove, or disinvest in, many treatments altogether. Effectiveness issues are rarely black and white. Even the government acknowledges the complexity and individualized nature of modern medicine.

Advocates of EBM caution against having unrealistic expectations of what it can deliver. For instance, Sir John Scott, a leading medical academic in New Zealand, comments that despite the fact that he has been preaching the doctrine of EBM for the past 35 years he is now more realistic about the benefits (St John 1997). He claims that the cost of producing and continually updating clinical guidelines is all too often overlooked. 'The hope that EBM will result in diminished costs is seen as the mirage which it potentially is' (St John 1997). Sir John is also critical of what he sees as a tendency to hold health professionals responsible for what are fundamentally faults within the system and its financial structure.

Regardless of the technical state of our knowledge as to what is or is not effective, a major issue centres on whether or not an ability exists to act on the evidence. So far, as was pointed out in Chapter 4, few health authorities have explicitly and absolutely excluded purchasing services although restrictions may govern the availability of some of them. Even those health authorities which have moved to exclude treat-ments have restricted their actions to services which are somewhat rare and of a specialized, even non-essential, nature. They are marginal to mainstream medicine. As such, their cost implications are not so significant when taken as a proportion of the budget as a whole. Services which have been excluded or, to be more precise, are not normally purchased, include those listed in Chapter 4, Box 4.2.

The government's view, supported by the British Medical Association, is that no treatments should be excluded even if in a given year they may not be available. But given the individual nature of clinical care, 'one should never say never' (Dr Sandy Macara, BMA, quoted in House of Commons Health Committee 1995a: para. 103, xxxiii). An issue for government is how much variation and diversity are tolerable in a service which is ostensibly national in character and coverage. A former Secretary of State for Health told the Health Committee that the government sought 'a balance between a national service accountable to Parliament which has the ability to have local flexibility and local initiatives and the diversity which is vital' (House of Commons Health Committee 1995a: para. 107, xxxiv). However, the fact that specific services may be available in one geographical area but not in another does raise issues of equity, access to care, and to accusations that the NHS is failing its commitment to be a *national* service providing comprehensive care. Although part of the problem here relates to the issue of explicitness, which will be considered later in the chapter, another part of it resides in the issue of effectiveness and the extent to which available evidence provides practical guidance in the appropriate use of services. Indeed, applying evidence is regarded as a more appropriate approach than a rigid exclusion policy. The Health Committee (House of Commons 1995a: para. 117, xxvi) defined appropriateness in the following terms: '[the use of services] which bases the choice of service on a knowledge of the likely effectiveness of that service or treatment, combined with a knowledge of the individual patient's condition and clinical history – in short, selecting the right service for the right patient'. The cost criterion was only taken into account when the effectiveness criterion had been satisfied. Variations in what is available are therefore likely to result from the notion of appropriateness. A further aspect of the variation problem should, however, be mentioned. Variation is to a large extent a feature of medical practice and clinical judgement which has always been present in the NHS, and, indeed, in health-care systems elsewhere.

Whatever the failings, limitations or gaps in the evidence, acting (or not acting) on it is a critical issue which raises the matter of managers' responsibility and competence, and the interface between management and medicine. The Health Committee noted the difficulties in this area and the ignorance which prevailed about how clinicians currently made decisions and used evidence. The difficulties centred on doctors being confronted by individual patients whom they were duty-bound to help. Such depictions of the reality of providing care as opposed to abstract conceptions of the process serve as a salutary reminder of the limits to clinical guidelines and protocols which can certainly serve as frameworks for decision-making but cannot be slavishly followed on the grounds that few procedures are totally ineffective. The Health Committee, after weighing the evidence, recommended that clinicians should be required to justify deviations from informed best practice and that persuasion not coercion should be the means employed to change clinical behaviour. As was noted in Chapter 2, the issue of managerial competence cannot be overlooked or lightly dismissed since it is all too easy to make the absence or weakness of evidence an excuse for management inaction or failure. Moreover, as was pointed out in Chapter 4, the current performance management or regulatory framework creates a perverse incentive which militates against an R&D culture developing within the purchasing function. At best, progress will be slow and probably patchy.

Voluntary restraint

There are a number of ways of viewing this policy option. Voluntary restraint can be exercised on the part of clinicians or on the part of patients. In the case of the former, clinicians may be discouraged from seeking to do all that is possible technically for a patient if, for instance, there are good grounds for believing that the patient is unlikely to benefit clinically, possibly on grounds of age or lifestyle (e.g. the patient is a heavy smoker). Obviously such restraint must be open to defence on clinical grounds and not on social or ethical ones, since the latter are not admissable.

In terms of voluntary restraint being exercised by patients, the argument here is that patients are in favour of treatment if it will enhance their quality of life but not at any price. They do not want medicine to be meddlesome or to render their quality of life so poor that it becomes a case not so much of living but of surviving. At stake is the amount, type and quality of the information made available to patients. Involving patients more fully in the choices about their own treatment might usefully be encouraged. Much of the information to be made available is fairly basic but it does not happen often or systematically enough. This issue touches on an important dimension of the preferred policy option – muddling through elegantly – to be explored later.

Another dimension of voluntary restraint is the fostering of self-help (Coote and Hunter 1996). Its value in promoting better health and health care should not be overlooked or underestimated. Self-help groups share a commitment to promoting autonomy and self-determination. Self-help is about personal responsibility and interdependence and people doing things for themselves rather than relying exclusively on statutory provision like health-care services. In many cases, patients may not want the invasive, costly, long-term treatment doctors think they would like or wish to inflict, preferring instead more self-management of their condition.

Explicit rationing

A preference for explicit rationing underlies, if not drives, a substantial part of the rationing debate. As has been argued, the heart of the matter is not that rationing is something new – it isn't – rather, it is the shifting nature of the debate which has changed. Whereas up until the 1991 NHS changes rationing received little public attention because decisions were ostensibly made on clinical grounds and could not therefore strictly be termed rationing decisions in the sense that some people were being denied effective interventions which they needed (as opposed to wanted or demanded), the arrival of market-style transactions with their currency of contracts, combined with the rise of managerialism at the expense of professional power, began to undermine received practices and the prevailing *modus operandi*. But with the genie well and truly out of the bottle and rationing, according to proponents of explicit rationing, occurring in all kinds of haphazard and variable ways which are unsatisfactory and indefensible in a *national* service, national leadership is urgently required to sort out the mess and inject much-needed rationality.

Given that much of decision-making in any sphere is messy and imprecise it is puzzling why health-care rationing has been singled out for special treatment from those – principally health economists (although there are some exceptions like Mullen (1995) and Coast (1997)) and health-services researchers – who wish to purify the decision process and make it both more rational (i.e. less messy) and scientific (i.e. based on hard evidence of what works and at what cost). If they are not intent on depoliticizing the making of choices they certainly want to keep politics at bay. This amounts to something of a paradox because their commitment to an explicit approach is based on a belief that there is already too much secrecy in British public life and that greater public involvement is both desirable and overdue (Doyal 1997).

Typical of the genre is an editorial in the *British Medical Journal* by Alan Maynard, former director of the Centre for Health Economics, University of York. But it is one of a growing list of similar pieces which the *BMJ* and some other outlets, notably *The Guardian* newspaper, regularly publish presumably in the hope that if the same message is repeated often enough it will over time make the government change its mind or eventually wear it down like a tap dripping on to a stone. The essence of the problem for Maynard (1996: 1499) is this: 'There seems to be a consensus that rationing is ubiquitous in all health care systems, yet in no country is there a clear and publicly accepted set of principles that can determine who gets what health care and when.' The NHS's budget is at the disposal of clinicians principally who are given discretion to 'do their own thing', rationing care by rules that differ and are incoherent and implicit. The sin that is committed by this offence is that inefficiency and inequity are rife although it is nowhere stated how a different system, even assuming public agreement would be forthcoming, would be less inefficient and inequitable. It could end-up being just as inefficient and inequitable albeit in a different way.

Maynard is dismissive of the literature on rights, citizens' juries and the proposal for a national priority committee or commission as being of no consequence in the absence of a clear explicit set of principles.

By these Maynard means socially agreed (though by which route is not spelled out) criteria that would determine access to limited NHS care. Such criteria would include agreement over the point at which it would no longer be appropriate to allocate resources to elderly people regardless of whether or not they might individually benefit from such a strategy in order to direct more resources towards young people who had their lives before them. But, as was pointed out in Chapter 2, age discrimination is generally regarded as unacceptable. This view is likely to become stronger as demographic trends result in an older population with the potential to exercise greater political influence and help shape social and health policy.

If rationing is to be explicit and underpinned by a set of publicly agreed principles, then there are a number of variations on this particular theme which were all considered in the context of other countries' experiences in Chapter 5. At one end of the spectrum there would be very tight criteria governing services to be included (and conversely excluded). This is the core service, or restricted menu, or limited list approach. It is sometimes known as the guaranteed entitlement to health care and has, in most countries, been found wanting. It has survived, though modified over time, in Oregon but the circumstances prevailing there are particular to the US so cannot be the basis of a useful comparison with the UK. Also, even in Oregon the process has been subjected to a degree of political manipulation which is at odds with its proclaimed scientific and publicly focused approach. New Zealand, where a core-service approach was attempted, quickly came to the view that such an approach could not be made to work or be made politically acceptable.

At the other extreme is the ethically sound approach. This does not seek to exclude any particular services or treatments but rather to establish a framework of ethics or principles which would guide, though not prescribe, decision-making over who should and should not receive treatment. Sweden is the best example of this approach but it is dismissed by the hard men (and it *is* men) of rationing who favour hard choices and regard the Swedish 'ethical platform' as vague, insufficiently precise to operationalize and ducking the difficult choices that must be made. In between these extremes are various approaches, notably the Dutch one, which seeks to combine elements of both approaches: the soft approach to defining and gaining public acceptance for a set of principles to assist in the making of choices, and the hard approach involving the making of specific decisions about who should get treatment (and by definition, if resources are limited, who should be denied it).

Another middle way, and one favoured by the UK and being taken up elsewhere, is to firm-up on the evidence base and to refuse to talk of rationing but, instead, use the term priority-setting. This, it is claimed, is not just semantics but makes an important distinction. Whereas rationing may entail the denial of a treatment regardless of its effectiveness simply because there is not enough to go round, priority-setting is much more concerned with choosing on the basis of what is effective and works. As long as ineffective procedures are being provided, it is wrong, or at the least premature, to talk of rationing. There is a prior need to terminate ineffective medical interventions. This is the view of the anti-rationing group led by Colin Roberts and colleagues based in Wales (Roberts *et al.* 1995).

The UK approach, as described in Chapter 4, is to favour clinical effectiveness and evidence-based medicine interventions which will not only demonstrate effective procedures but also what needs to happen to change clinical behaviour. The approach is not a heavy handed top–down one but is being pursued through persuasion and an R&D strategy which sets great store by the production of good evidence and knowledge in which clinicians and others can have respect. Indeed, they may even have helped contribute to the accumulation of knowledge. Such a strategy involves a long haul and will not yield quick results. Moreover, a scientific, expert approach of this nature can be alienating from the public's point of view and can serve to depoliticize, and lend a spurious scientific objectivity to, what are largely subjective, value-based matters for decision. This is a curious paradox when the government is seeking at the same time to include the public as active contributors to priority-setting. Arguably, this will become more difficult to achieve as the scientific base is strengthened – unless what we think of as science and as constituting evidence changes and moves away from its entrenched biomedical bias (Dean and Hunter 1996).

Explicit rationing sounds fine in theory – who could possibly be against it in an ideal world? But the world is not ideal. It is messy, turbulent, ambivalent and, as Handy notes, full of paradox which is 'inevitable, endemic, and perpetual' (Handy 1994: 17). The trick is not to seek to eliminate paradox but rather to manage it. Unfortunately this subtle distinction appears lost on the advocates of rational rationing who yearn for clarity, precision and certainty. Hard choices is what it is all about – not fudge, compromise and a blurring of the issues. That way lies inefficiency and inequity and, they assert, ultimately the collapse of the NHS. This argument seems to ignore completely the obvious: namely, that politicians may neither wish to make, nor be capable of making, the hard choices that are apparently so necessary and unavoidable. What if explicit rationing is not possible, either for political or other reasons and, in fact, suffers from severe pitfalls which far from making it desirable may render it counter-productive and even harmful? And what if it is actually so difficult to do that it becomes a distraction from other important aspects of health-care policy? After all, the give-away phrase in Maynard's *BMJ* editorial cited above is that 'in no country is there a clear and publicly accepted set of principles that can determine who gets what health care and when' (Maynard, 1996). But, as the review of selected experiences in Chapter 5 demonstrated, this is not for want of trying, although Maynard conveniently omits this fact. Several countries, as described in the last chapter, have struggled with such a task and have either abandoned it, transformed the problem into a different one, or have failed to implement it in a ruthless, utilitarian manner, thereby being guilty of ducking the hard choices. Surely the fact that countries have tried and not yet succeeded is a crucial piece of evidence which merits careful study and analysis. Perhaps explicit rationing could only be achieved at too high a price politically. The pitfalls of explicit rationing may simply have become too great. They are reviewed next.

The pitfalls of explicit rationing

Five pitfalls merit comment in the various attempts to make rationing more explicit. They are:

- whose voice?
- the quality of decision-making
- the power of numbers
- underfunding is the issue
- when does covert become overt and vice versa?

Some of them have already been referred to earlier.

Whose voice?

Uppermost in any discussion about rationing is the question of whose voice is being articulated when public opinion is sought on issues like establishing priorities in health care? Is it the articulate middle class in a local community? Is it the 'worried well', whose perceptions of health services differ markedly from those of the long-term chronic sick? Explicit rationing that is based on seeking the public's views carries the danger of a low priority being attached to the needs of people with a mental illness, a mental handicap, a physical disability, those who are old and those who may be poor and inarticulate. Who will act as advocates on their behalf? Do the media have a role in informing the public and promoting debate? Is their purpose educational or sensational?

Participation is inherently inegalitarian. The question, therefore, is the extent to which it should be relied on in rationing health care. And if it is not relied on, what is its purpose or value? While arguing in favour of greater public participation Doyal and Gough (1991) warn that 'It can advantage the already privileged through their ability to manipulate the information process and can sacrifice the common good to sectional interpretations of it.' A pilot project conducted in Leeds which sought to discover what local people themselves thought they needed in the way of health and social services found that it was extremely hard to reach certain groups in the community, in particular Asian women (Percy-Smith and Sanderson 1992). It was also difficult to get any but a few 'regulars' to turn up to open meetings. The exercise was expensive and time-consuming which, even if useful, is doubtless a factor which will weigh with cost-conscious health authorities especially when the novelty of consulting the public has worn off. Indeed, as Coote (1993: 41) states, consultation if thorough 'doesn't come cheap'. At a time when downward pressure on management costs in the NHS is intensifying, this has to be an important factor to take into account. The study referred to earlier on the costs of commissioning reports that in respect of the medium-term priority of giving greater voice and influence to users of the NHS, health authorities spend an average 30p per head, or 3 per cent of their total costs. GP purchasers spend a similar percentage (Griffiths 1996).

Consultation can be an effective way of feeding the views of the public (as citizens or customers) into decisions about rationing. How effective it is, from the 'public's' point of view, depends on what questions are asked, by whom, of whom, by what means and on the basis of what information; on whether any dialogue takes place and, if so, with whom; on how the answers are processed and conclusions drawn, and what action is taken as a result. As Coote (1993) points out, all these decisions remain in the hands of those who consult – as is the decision whether or not to consult in the first place. 'At worst, it can be a highly manipulative process benefiting no one but the consulting body. At best, it can be a route towards more open and appropriate decisions, more enlightened decision-making and a better-informed public' (Coote 1993: 40–1).

Implicit rationing is criticized on the grounds that, as Mechanic (1995: 1657) puts it, 'Knowledgeable, sophisticated, and aggressive patients are more able to have their needs satisfied than docile patients.' But in fact explicit rationing can give rise to a similar bias – indeed, it is perhaps a more likely outcome in the absence of any advocate for the patient who may be able to argue their case successfully. The articulate middle-class consumer is likely, through explicit rationing and public involvement in it, to have their views heard at the expense of the less articulate or assertive.

If we are serious about encouraging people to participate actively in health-care rationing decisions then we need to give proper attention to preparing people for such a role and to providing sufficient information to aid and inform the choices they will be required to make. A responsible media approach to these difficult and complex issues is also required if reasoned debate is to be promoted in place of high emotion. A system of procedural rights may also assist in ensuring greater fairness and explicitness at the level of individual care (see below).

A concern must be that many of those championing public involvement are not in fact truly seeking to empower people in order to enable them to participate effectively but rather may be seeking a superficial legitimacy – a veneer – for what would remain essentially management decisions about priorities. Painful choices and trade-offs would then become conveniently diffused in the process and no longer appear to fall to professionals and managers alone. Managers feel especially uncomfortable with being made responsible for such decisions because they neither possess the technical expertise nor have the confidence of the public in making such decisions legitimately or in an accountable manner. Being accountable in this context means locally, i.e. downwards to communities rather than upwards to ministers and Parliament.

But public involvement in a complex area like health care poses other challenges and risks. Whether we approve of it or not, our education system and employment structures do not prepare people for a high level of political involvement in matters which directly affect them or provide them with opportunities and support to enable them actively to participate, or equip them with the skills to do so. Indeed, quite the opposite is invariably the case with the consequence that people are, for the most part, passive bystanders. Correcting this major lacuna in our societal functioning would seem to be an essential prerequisite for effec-tive, explicit rationing in health care in which at least the attempt is made to create a level playing-field in order to allow involvement from *all* sections of the public and not just those self-selected by the decibel level. Even then we will be asking a lot of the public to be involved in the rationing debate. Do we know whether, and to what extent, people really want to be actively involved? And how practicable is it to expect involvement without providing people with a considerable amount of background information and context? This is not to argue against the principle of encouraging greater public involvement but there is a need to be realistic about what it will achieve. Moreover, if we are truly in favour of people power then we may need to accept *greater* variation in health care rather than less. Herein lies another paradox because many of those who are concerned about the extent of variation are among the staunchest supporters of public involvement.

Traditionally, reliance has been placed on health-care professionals, principally clinicians, not merely to ration health care but also to act as advocates on behalf of certain groups whose interests and preferences may not otherwise receive adequate representation. There is a tension in doctors, especially GPs, acting as advocates on the one hand and gate-keepers or resource-managers on the other. Mechanic (1984) argues that resource constraints have transformed the doctor–patient relationship. The needs of an individual patient must be weighed against those of others. Doctors are required not only to look after the individual patient but also the whole community. In short, they must adopt a community-oriented approach for which they must be held accountable. In this may lie the key to resolving the doctors' dilemma over their role in rationing. In its statement of core values for the medical profession in the twenty-first century, the BMA includes among the core values the following:

Community responsibility requires doctors to take part in wider formal discussions on priorities and ensure that the public can make informed contributions. However, there will be occasions when the doctor's primary responsibility to individual patients conflicts with wider community responsibilities. In these circumstances, the individual doctor's duty of care is to individual patients.

(BMA 1995b: 14)

What is important to stress is that the scope for improving current arrangements may be preferable to a wholesale shift to public involvement at any or every level of rationing – macro, meso and micro – but especially at the meso and micro levels. This is perhaps especially so when 'the public' is not the uniform, homogeneous monolithic entity implied by the term or thought to exist by some commentators and policy-makers. The challenge involved in making that voice, or those voices, effectively heard or articulated may be beyond our grasp and remain an unachievable and illusory aspiration. The media have not, for the most part, proved themselves to be sufficiently responsible to take on the task. For instance, in a study of the Kendrick case (a patient denied treatment for renal cell carcinoma because of lack of funds) Freemantle (1994) examines the role played by the popular press in its handling of the affair. He concludes that the press on this occasion neither informed the public nor stimulated a debate. Rather, it purveyed in rather typical fashion 'shroud-waving myth'. Coverage in the popular press took for granted, and was underpinned by, the dominant medical model even when the treatment in question was of dubious efficacy. The quality press probably cannot be relied on to do much better.

The quality of decision-making

There must surely be concern over the impact of rationing, if it becomes more explicit, on the quality of decision-making. For instance, will it lead to more incremental and conservative decisions at the risk of preventing the development of innovative or different patterns of delivery? It is possible that reallocating resources from, say, acute to community care or long-term care, difficult though this has been to achieve, could become even more difficult when processes which have been implicit become explicit. Merely by increasing the visibility of a decision process, and allowing many more individuals and groups access to it, the potential for conflict among key groups of decision-makers is likely to increase (Mechanic 1995). The example given above of the Kendrick case would seem to confirm the view that a conservative approach would prevail.

If managers are being exhorted by the government to switch priorities to the long-term care groups and away from acute services on the one hand while the opposite message is coming from public consultation and the popular press on the other, how do managers decide to advance? The difficulties may be compounded if evidence-based medicine suggests one course of action which may run counter to expressed public preferences. In such a situation, the action taken may actually be to take as little action as possible and to preserve current patterns of service.

The choice comes down to one of maintaining the virtues and strengths of an essentially paternalistic system (but one that must nevertheless undergo change – see below) in preference to one which, though more visible, could actually hamper decision-making. As Klein (1992a: 5) has put it:

the greater the visibility of rationing in the sense of prioritisation, the more difficult it may become to steer resources towards the most vulnerable ... groups. Lack of visibility may be a necessary condition for the political paternalism required to overcome both consumer and producer lobbies.

This line of reasoning might suggest the merits of strengthening democratic control over the NHS possibly in the form of a reinvigorated local government and a fresh approach to the issue of governance (see below).

There is a parallel between the visibility versus invisibility issue in rationing with attempts in the 1970s to make the management of central government more rational and efficient (Heclo and Wildavsky 1981). Management techniques, like programme planning and budgeting, and programme analysis and review, were introduced to make central government departments more open and transparent about their priorities and the resources available to meet them. But increased openness and explicitness, although reducing the scope for backstairs deals between various interests, actually reinforced, even actively encouraged, incrementalism and made it more difficult to depart from the historical base. Paradoxically, incrementalism was reinforced by the new techniques, making each department more conscious of its own fair share of the total and more aware of other departments' departures from the expected rate of increase. Being explicit served to focus conflict and dissatisfaction. The point about this example is that devices or procedures introduced with one objective in view can result in quite unanticipated, and probably unintended, consequences which may in fact make the achievement of the original objective more difficult or virtually impossible. Such devices and procedures cannot be viewed in isolation from the context into which they are introduced.

The power of numbers

Coast (1997: 1120) argues that explicit rationing can give rise to two sources of disutility: (a) citizens become involved in the process of denying care to particular groups of individuals, or particular individuals may experience disutility – 'denial disutility'; (b) disutility may arise when individuals are informed explicitly that their care is being rationed – 'deprivation disutility'. Both types of disutility may be distressing, therefore the clinical benefits of explicitness may be less than expected: 'explicitness may be unable to generate the sets of principles which lead to improved decising-making. Even if such principles can be generated, it may not be possible to sustain the explicit decisions which follow' (p. 1121). In Coast's view, explicitness carries its own disutility which may outweigh any 'benefit' in moving from an implicit to an explicit approach. 'In this situation, the openness and honesty of explicitness may be too great a burden to bear compared with the equivocation associated with implicit rationing' (Coast 1997). As we saw in the case of QALYs (Chapter 4), numbers can have a curiously mesmerizing effect on managers and others required to produce and rely on them. Often, unfounded assumptions of certainty and precision seem to underpin the very hardness of numbers. Once complex problems and decisions on them have been reduced to simple quantifiable comparisons of costs and benefits or some kind of quality index (like QALYs) it seems quite irrational not to act in accordance with the numbers. But, as was pointed out in Chapter 4, this is a cause for concern because index numbers are not an observation of real life: they are generated and produced by a specific set of technical procedures which may be more or less comprehensible to the average manager or non-executive director. It is all too easy to forget the value base of numbers and to attach a degree of certainty and precision to them that may be quite unfounded or unwarranted (Carr-Hill 1989; Carr-Hill and Sheldon 1992). Cost-utility approaches, like QALYs, are riddled with dangers of this kind for the unwary. While there may be a place for such techniques in the decision process, they surely cannot be major determinants of it or seek to supplant other, perhaps softer, measures of quality.

Underfunding is the issue

The issue of underfunding has already been examined earlier in this chapter so will not be dwelt on at length here. While in the Oregon experiment, the move to explicit rationing was intended to demonstrate deficiencies or gaps in services or an inability to fund adequate care in the hope that this would put pressure on policy-makers to devote more resources to health care, it is possible that the opposite is equally true. Explicit rationing, especially in the form of a restricted list or core-service approach, could lead policy-makers to believe that there is some finite level of health care and level of resources that are appropriate. Arguments for devoting additional resources to health care would then receive short shrift.

When does covert become overt (and vice versa)?

There is a danger of duplicity or of a dual standard developing whereby covert rationing simply continues under the guise of overt rationing. Professionals are adept at 'gaming the system' to suit their interests. There is ample evidence from the US to show that when diagnosis-related groups (DRGs) were introduced, clinicians quickly became skilled at fitting patients to the various groups and categories of care. It is a process known as 'DRG creep'. Similarly, under a system of rationing where some procedures are permissible and others are not, it would be quite possible to ensure that all patients were treated by making them fit the various categories that had been devised. The point is that under the pretext of an explicit and rational rationing system, implicit rationing could continue to occur with one important difference: namely, that it would be even further hidden from view since it would no longer be assumed to be taking place.

At issue is the fact that, as Mechanic (1995: 1658) puts it, 'The assumption that explicit rules are inviolable is . . . unrealistic.' He cites an observed instance of the allocation committee for kidney dialysis being bypassed to accommodate a patient. Mechanic concludes from this episode that 'The rich and powerful if sufficiently motivated will always find ways to circumvent explicit criteria.'

Having in effect a dual overt and covert system of rationing operating in tandem would be disastrous and result in even greater inequities than those now in evidence. Under an implicit arrangement there is at least an awareness that rationing decisions are taken by various professionals and even if such a system attracts a degree of disapproval because it is seen as closed and obscure, repeated public opinion surveys demonstrate that people prefer and, most important, have trust in this arrangement. Any other alternative would require a dramatic departure from it. If there was to be a move towards an explicit rationing system, or at any rate towards one which was presented as such, there is a danger of the public being misled into thinking it is making, or contributing to, decisions when in fact it may not be at all or only rarely. If this were to occur, and worse be shown to occur, it would surely seriously undermine any faith in an explicit approach. Certainly, trust in such an arrangement would evaporate. As was pointed out in Chapter 4, trust is an important and rare commodity in the smooth conduct of relationships in the NHS and is already under threat as a consequence of the market-style changes ushered in in 1991.

An assessment

These observations on possible pitfalls arising from moves to establish a form of explicit rationing are not intended to imply an uncritical and essentially conservative defence of the current system which is often crtiticized for being grounded in professional paternalism (which may be giving way at the margins to a form of managerial paternalism). Rather, their intention is to demonstrate the need for a more realistic and sophisticated assessment of the complexities involved in switching from a form of implicit to explicit rationing and the possible implications, intended or otherwise, of such a development. If advocates of an explicit approach believe human behaviour under an implicit approach to be irrational, what and where is the evidence for believing it will be any different (and presumably better) under an explicit system?

One Director of Public Health, Ron Zimmern, has questioned the current received wisdom that it is now necessary to make transparent and explicit all decisions within clinical and commissioning spheres and that such explicitness is both effective and appropriate. While there is much to commend such a view, Zimmern (1996) cautions against being as certain about its advantages. He supports those who have questioned the wisdom of too much explicitness, arguing that while patient autonomy and rights might be strengthened, their welfare could at the same time be compromised.

But Zimmern does not cite these arguments in order to return to an unsatisfactory medical paternalism but to show that the issues are rather more complex than is often asserted to be the case. There is, as Zimmern puts it, 'another side to the views that prevail at present and which should be taken into account if we are to make the necessary initial judgements about how best to optimise the health and welfare of our patients'. Zimmern's views are even more interesting when we consider that he is Director of Public Health for Cambridge and Huntingdon Health Commission which handled the Child B case (see Chapter 1, Box 1.1).

(Masterly) inactivity

The last of the policy options to be considered, before moving on to describe the preferred option, may be termed (masterly) inactivity. It is invariably the preferred choice of government ministers and officials, particularly when confronted by a minefield which health-care rationing must surely be on all fronts. In many ways, the present policy of devolving responsibility for rationing to health authorities, trusts and GPs has the hallmarks of a policy of inactivity since the centre resists getting involved in individual clinical cases. Moreover, managers working with clinicians and others have the job of setting priorities but tend to do so in ways which do not disturb the *status quo*. To this extent, then, the *status quo* is maintained and a general stratagem of muddling through is evident. This is certainly the picture which emerges from the analysis of Roberts *et al.* (1995) of the current inability of managers to manage clinical resources effectively which, if they did, would obviate the need to ration health care. Inactivity and a strategy of policy maintenance results from a combination of resistance among practitioners, the existence of vested interests pursuing protectionist policies, weak management in the midst of these forces and pressures, and frequent political interference despite the rhetoric of decentralized responsibility.

But it would not be fair to characterize official policy as an example *par excellence* of inactivity, masterly or otherwise, since there has been an active commitment to knowledge-based health care by investing in the evidence-based medicine movement and related notions like clinical effectiveness and guidelines/protocols (see Chapter 4). The official policy is for health authorities and trusts and those working in primary health care to invest in procedures known to be effective and to disinvest in those where the evidence suggests they are ineffective (NHS Executive 1996). What is missing is any link between these exhortations and the performance-management system for holding health authorities and GPs to account.

While a policy of muddling through has much to commend it given the problems surrounding efforts to establish all the rules beforehand (Mechanic 1995), attention needs to be given to how such a policy can perhaps be made a little less imperfect – that is, not merely muddling through, but *muddling through elegantly*. This is the preferred policy option for reasons described in the next subsection.

Muddling through elegantly

If overt explicit rationing is such a minefield strewn with major problems each one potentially explosive then why pursue it in such dogged fashion? Why should those of a particular mind set and view of rationality hold sway and seek to monopolize the argument and public debate? Why not consider adopting a rather more subtle and incremental approach which acknowledges the complexities of real-life priority-setting and the 'wicked' problem that it is? Such an approach, aimed at arriving at an optimal balance between various interests, has been termed 'muddling through elegantly' (Hunter 1993a).

Greater transparency, including effective public involvement, in rationing decisions ought to be encouraged where, and in ways that are, appropriate but it needs to be buttressed and supported, in particular by not allowing professionals to evade their clinical responsibilities to individuals and groups in need of support. They should not, as many would prefer to do, opt out of the dialogue over rationing altogether, leaving it entirely to managers, politicians and the public to make their own judgements, possibly on the basis of poor or incomplete information, and in ways which risk favouring some sections of the community over others. At the same time, professionals must not be allowed to set the agenda over priorities on the basis of their preferences alone, especially when these are socially rather than clinically based. In making the transition from 'advocacy to allocation' (Mechanic 1986), where the doctor must balance the patient's needs against the need for cost control, doctors must be key actors in the decision process alongside other groups including users. The problem of rationing only becomes one for doctors when they adhere rigidly to an advocacy stance on behalf of individual patients and remain unaccountable for their actions to the wider community. As allocators of resources, regardless of whether or not they hold actual budgets, doctors must be held publicly accountable since their actions will affect groups of people directly as well as individuals.

As has been shown, rationing is a multifaceted and multilevelled activity and needs to be tackled accordingly. Hence the attractions of a muddling through approach which, far from being indefensible and defeatist, acknowledges the dynamic nature of rationing, its complexities and its subtleties. The approach is well suited to situations of extreme uncertainty, paradox and complexity (even multiplexity) where information is poor, incomplete and often contested. Although it is a feature of all health-care systems, the centrality of rationing to policy debates is variable and depends, *inter alia*, on the acuteness of resource pressures prevailing at any particular point in time. If we are to find, and agree on, the appropriate policy response then we need to consider what rationing means at different levels and agree on who needs to be involved at each level and through what means.

As was noted in Chapter 2, there are five levels of rationing. The first level is concerned with deciding how much to allocate to health care as against competing demands on public resources such as education, housing and social security, all of which may contribute as much, if not more, to the population's health status as health services. The second level of rationing is determining how to split the total budget among different priorities or care groups. For instance, should heart surgery take precedence over general medicine? Or should hip-joint replacements take precedence over intensive care baby units? The third level is deciding priorities *within* services. The fourth and final levels involve decisions about how to use the resources available: namely, which particular patients to treat, when and how and to what level of intensity, and which ones not to treat.

If there is a place for a public debate about rationing it is surely at the first level. Many observers would argue that the public should be involved at the first four levels while a few would wish to see involvement at all five levels covering macro, meso and micro decisions – but there are major difficulties in doing so. Professional opinion and input is crucial at all levels but especially at levels four and five. Most attempts to engage the public at a health authority level have centred on the second level: that is, deciding priorities between different care groups or activities. But devising appropriate mechanisms for putting rationing options to the public is fraught with difficulties. There is a particular threat to the notion of 'common goods' or 'collective provision' which is the glue holding the NHS together. Widening the debate about rationing could give rise to a new individualism or narrow utilitarianism which may weaken the collectivist ethos which underpins the NHS. There is a paradox in all of this since a utilitarian perspective aims at putting the collective good before the individual good but, it is argued here, any attempt to do so is likely to destroy the very solidarity and collectivist ethos a utilitarian approach seeks to uphold. Some balance between the two poles of collectivism and individualism is desirable. It has been suggested that a system of procedural rights to ensure that individuals are dealt with fairly would put in place a set of clear principles to be observed in order that the decision-making process and any expert discretion involved were made explicit (Coote and Hunter 1996; Lenaghan 1996).

Procedural rights are rights to the fair treatment (in the non-clinical sense) of individuals as they come into contact, or try to come into contact, with service providers. The NHS has in fact gone some way towards a rights-based approach in this sense. The introduction of the *Patient's Charter*, corporate governance codes, the *Openness Code*, new powers for the Health Service Commissioner and a strong complaints system all carry it further in this direction. But there is still a long way yet to travel since the *Patient's Charter*'s so-called 'rights' are not enforceable. A system of procedural rights *could* ensure *fair dealing* between providers and users but it would need to avoid curtailing professional discretion where this is deemed appropriate and which is a cornerstone of muddling through elegantly.

A possible starting point for such a rights-based approach would be to develop guidelines about how decisions are made and by whom (Coote and Hunter 1996). Such guidelines could be developed nationally or, perhaps preferably, locally by elected bodies. Either way, health authorities would be obliged to follow the guidelines. The guidelines would not, however, dictate which treatments are available or which ones are ruled out. Rather, they should structure the way in which decisions are made and ensure greater transparency. Health authorities and trusts, clinicians and managers would abide by a shared set of criteria and procedures but would not be shackled by these. A public commission has been proposed to advise Parliament on devising the guidelines (Lenaghan 1996) but the drawback with this proposal is that a commission might become an expert group of the 'good and the great' with the odd token patient or consumer. Such a body could well end up displaying the very remoteness, paternalism and élitism so despised by ardent advocates of people power – at outcome which is not so different from that which a procedural rights-based approach seeks to overturn. Citizens' juries, discussed in Chapter 4, might also be piloted as a means of providing an input from the general public. Juries and other forms of participatory democracy would, however, in terms of our preferred option complement rather than substitute for representative democracy which itself needs strengthening to counter the charge of a 'democratic deficit' in the NHS. We return to this subject below.

It is important to emphasize that the procedural guidelines proposed for the NHS would not amount to a guide to rationing for the simple reason, as other countries' experience has shown (and there is no reason whatsoever for believing the UK is any different on this score), that politicians will always resist attempts to make specific, explicit judgements about what to exclude or include by way of the treatments on offer. Any guidelines which are primarily about rationing are therefore likely to be so general, vacuous and ultimately trivial as to be of limited usefulness. The guidelines discussed here would have a quite different purpose. They would endeavour to establish a set of general principles expressing, or rather restating since they already exist, the values and objectives of the NHS and setting standards for fair and consistent administrative procedures. Much of the groundwork has already been done but various discrete initiatives and practices need to be brought together into a simple coherent and comprehensible framework and preferably without drama or fuss. Within this overarching framework implicit rationing would occur at a micro level.

Why should fair treatment be important? And how is this principle to be balanced alongside the principle of permitting the exercise of discretion where appropriate? Bynoe (1996: 84) explains the position thus:

> If entitlement to many services is to remain a matter largely for the exercise of discretion, not the application of detailed regulation, then measures designed to 'structure' the use of discretion and guarantee its fair application will become all the more important if principles of equity and equal treatment are to be respected.

Fair treatment is an important mark of quality, especially in a public service which professes to be *national* in character, and 'a factor affecting the long-term future of the public's relationship with services which they vote and pay for, since people will trust and value services they judge to be fairly administered'. Procedural rights in health care may be summarized as follows (Bynoe 1996):

- *a right to be heard:* a right for someone to be consulted, on the basis of shared information, by a person or body making a decision which affects their circumstances
- *a right to consistency in decision-making:* a right to treatment which is consistent with any established practice or promise
- *a right to relevance in decision-making:* a duty on those making decisions to take into account all relevant factors and to disregard irrelevant ones
- *a right to unbiased decisions:* a duty on those making decisions to act without bias
- *a right to reasons:* openness in decision-making, expressed as a requirement for the decision-maker to give reasons to those affected by decisions concerning them
- *a right to review:* the right to have the refusal of a service, or a complaint about one, independently reviewed.

These principles, many of which already exist in some form or to some degree, are no more than we would expect from good practice or well-developed clinical guidelines. They could be applied to all areas of health care, not rigidly or uniformly, but flexibly and adapted to suit the particular circumstances in which different forms of treatment and care are provided. Procedural rights of the type proposed would need to be enforced by a dedicated body such as the Health Service Commissioner (far preferable to setting up a new body for the purpose). Appeal to the courts would only occur as a last resort when all other avenues of redress had failed.

At a micro level – the fourth and fifth levels of rationing mentioned above – doctors and managers (but principally the former whose advice managers generally follow) make decisions about individual patients on a case-by-case basis, often involving a value-for-money assessment as well as purely clinical criteria. It is at these levels where most rationing takes place and where the most acute ethical and moral dilemmas can arise. Traditionally, rationing at these levels has always been implicit and no convincing reasons have yet been advanced to justify a change. But by implicit is not meant covert (as discussed earlier under 'pitfalls of explicit rationing') which implies secret protocols, lists of patient types or treatments which doctors and managers conspire to exclude without the public knowing. Secrecy has no place in implicit rationing but privacy and confidentiality do have a central place in the 'negotiated order' between doctor and patient and any significant others.

Nor can any predetermined rationing formula be applied. A basic health-care package for the NHS, or lists of excluded treatments published by health authorities, are crude and reductionist. This approach, if pursued, would only undermine or distort clinical judgement, leading to decisions which are insensitive to individual needs and circumstances (Coote and Hunter 1996). Moreover, it could have the effect, intended or unintended, of encouraging better-off people to leave the NHS and induce distrust and resentment among those who could not afford to do so.

But implicit micro-level rationing, which lies at the heart of muddling through elegantly, must observe certain disciplines and principles. For instance, clinicians and managers should be prepared to (Coote and Hunter 1996: 68–9):

- follow explicit guidance setting out broad indicative procedural criteria for decisions along the lines discussed above (these could emanate from national or local government, if health authorities merge with it, or be derived from clinical guidelines)
- improve the quality of their dialogue with patients, supplying full information on diagnosis, prognosis and options for treatment or non-treatment, including possible side effects and impact on quality of life
- defend any decision about an individual's treatment or exclusion if reasonably challenged by the patient or their representative.

It is conceivable that the passivity and paternalism still in evidence will progressively give way to a new relationship between doctors and patients with the latter enjoying greater collaboration, possibly on more equal terms, with providers. As more information becomes available and enters the public domain concerning clinical effectiveness and outcomes, much of it a direct result of the Internet and its potential to inform patients, then the power imbalance between patients and providers must surely shift in favour of the former. Inevitably, and rightly, providers' monopoly of information will be weakened and patients will demand, and have, more of a say. At a micro level, therefore, individual decisions seem likely in future to involve patients more directly. Tudor Hart (1994), himself a GP now retired, advocates recognition of patients as co-producers of their health rather than consumers. As co-producers, 'patients must share much more actively both in defining their problems and in devising feasible solutions than they have in the past' (p. 43). Tudor Hart believes that if patients were encouraged to play a more active part in their diagnosis and care then not only would more appropriate support be forthcoming but the savings from inappropriate referrals and interventions would be considerable. Recognition of patients as 'essential partners for health production' would also serve as a means of countering the rise of defensive medicine and clinical decisions prompted by fear of reprisals. The need for high-trust relations, which as we saw in an earlier chapter can all too easily be destroyed by markets and consumerism, is paramount in this redefined and rebalanced doctor–patient relationship. By definition it is an *implicit* relationship insofar as it excludes the wider community from any involvement in determining the outcome of the encounter. But it is an *explicit* and open relationship between doctor and patient. Indeed, it is an example in microcosm of a new participatory democracy developing, as Tudor Hart (1994) puts it, 'creative power at the periphery'. There are, in any such relationships, obligations on patients as well as doctors especially when it suits many patients to adopt a passive consumer role.

There is a link between the micro and meso levels which is well articulated by Tudor Hart (1994: 6) and worth quoting at length:

vesting all public responsibility for personal care in professionals effectively accountable to nobody ... must now be recognised as having become a fundamental constraint on future progress. Accountability to appointed, unelected managers has been a disaster. Health workers must be accountable to someone; why not to the people they serve? A critical mass of both health professionals and the public are now ready for a new era in health care, the transformation of patients from an essentially passive status as consumers, to become active co-producers of health gain. This sometimes glib concept could become an extremely powerful idea if it were translated into specific, concrete, practical clinical terms. This would open up new perspectives for local participatory democracy which would undo the damage done to the NHS by aggressive managerialism, without returning to the complacent stagnation of unaccountable professionalism.

The strength and appeal of a system of implicit rationing at a micro level, however imperfect it may be, is its attempt to balance individual with communal perspectives. To make the process any more explicit risks counterposing individual against collective well-being in a particularly stark form which has, in the words of one observer, 'enormous potential for mischief' (Rothman 1992). This truth is even recognized by at least some of the rational rationers. As New and Le Grand (1996: 69) concede, 'There is a very real danger that moving too fast in abandoning a system which has sustained the NHS for nearly 50 years could prove equally damaging.' And again: 'Attempts to be more systematic, efficient and democratic may not always result in anticipated improvements' (1996: 71). This leads New and Le Grand to conclude that, given the complex individualized nature of medicine, 'clinicians are inevitably going to be the final arbiters of individual rationing decisions, leaving national policies which seek to develop appropriate criteria for rationing at this "micro" level struggling to achieve anything of substance' (1996: 70).

There are clear dangers, too, in basing the provision of care on non-medical criteria, such as age and lifestyle, which would probably happen to an even greater extent than is the case now (see Chapter 2) if clinicians opted out and left rationing decisions to managers and the public through means not yet specified. It then becomes very easy to start blaming victims for their diseases and, where a link can be established, their socioeconomic status. Whatever unacceptable discriminatory practices currently occur through professional rationing (e.g. on grounds of age or lifestyle such as smoking or drug misuse) could be eclipsed by any move to more public forms of rationing.

None of this is to deny that rationing is at present imperfect. Indeed, it has been a key assumption underpinning this book that it most likely always will be since it represents a perfect example of those unwinnable dilemmas of social policy with which the book opened in Chapter 1. Given this reality, an appropriate philosophy for difficult decision-making might be one based on 'pragmatic sensibility' (Smith 1992: 59–60). Smith explains:

Pragmatism can . . . avoid the ethical traps of expediency and absolutism. The latter are often generated by the classical theories of utilitarianism and deontology. They are at fault in the changing world of modern medicine because they fail to offer solutions for the large number of permutations associated with human health.

Before becoming entangled, as we are in real danger of doing egged on by health economists, together with a handful of other academics and commentators, in a complex, and probably ultimately futile, quest for rational rationing through greater public involvement at each stage (and level) in the process there is surely a prior need to secure effectively managed health care through techniques like health-outcomes assessment, utilization review and quality improvement. If the NHS R&D initiative, and the EBM movement to which it has given birth, begin to grip as they must to some degree if they are to remain credible and justify the continuing investment of resources in them, then rationing health care through elaborate public consultation exercises, whose purpose is often muddled and confused, becomes not only unnecessary but also a cruel diversion from the real issues that urgently demand attention. Better information on health outcomes, and on what works and does not work, ought to inform decision-making in order that only interventions of proven efficacy, and/or where the health gain can be demonstrated, are funded. The scope for redeploying resources from ineffective and/or unnecessary procedures and practices is probably immense and, notwithstanding the constraints and limitations set out in

Chapter 4, may be a far more effective means of aiding rationing than imperfectly sampling public opinion. Moreover, the public's views about outcomes and measures of success ought to be a central component of the EBM movement. It should not be seen as the preserve of professionals alone. But for this to happen it will be necessary to relax the present bias towards biomedical research and to embrace a wider range of methodologies, notably the behavioural social sciences (Long and Eskin 1995; Dean and Hunter 1996).

We are still in the foothills as far as tackling these difficult issues is concerned (Wennberg 1990). Moreover, we must not overestimate the potential for EBM to serve as an antidote to rationing because it is unlikely ever to do so. With or without EBM, rationing seems inevitable especially in the short term since EBM will take some years to produce results and succeed in modifying clinician behaviour. Moreover, it will only do so if managers are prepared to make decisions on the basis of the evidence produced. This remains one of the weakest, yet most critical, areas in need of attention and could prove to be the downfall of the R&D initiative unless a research culture becomes central to, and embedded in, the management function. But EBM remains important because it offers a new perspective on rationing and imposes a discipline which demands *a priori* that the effectiveness of an intervention, where known, becomes the starting point for a discussion about the need for rationing. As Howell (1992) puts it, the two key questions centre (a) on the level of overall funding for the NHS and its adequacy given what the NHS is being asked to do and the apparent willingness of the public to invest more in it as a public service (as distinct from shifting to private provision), and (b) on ensuring that what is already allocated to the NHS is used prudently and effectively. Rationing, in Howell's view, should not be the issue and, more important, need not be.

If we return for a moment to the meso level of rationing, which represents a combination of the second and third levels noted earlier, there is one other avenue worthy of exploration in respect of public involvement in determining priorities. It was mentioned in the Tudor Hart quote cited above. The issue is not one of involving individual members of the public in some sort of exercise in direct democracy but concerns the nature of accountability at a community (i.e. health authority) level and of improving mechanisms for holding clinicians and managers to account for what they do and for the decisions they make on behalf of the communities they serve. Part of this refers back to the earlier discussion of rights but it also has implications for the public championing role of health authorities which would seem to demand changes in their composition and operation so that they more accurately reflect the local community. Arising from this, and as mentioned in Chapter 4, there may be a strong case for placing the health-authority function within local government thereby bringing it within the ambit of local representative democracy. The case for such a change has attracted a wide, and reasonably respectable, following (Harrison *et al.* 1991; Association of Metropolitan Authorities 1993; Clarke, Hunter and Wistow 1995, 1997; Cooper *et al.* 1995).

As we have insisted throughout, the delivery of health services is properly a matter for professionals operating at a micro level, in conjunction with patients as co-equal partners, but the commissioning of health services according to locally determined priorities, together with other public services which have an impact on health, is an appropriate matter for a publicly accountable, representative body. As Coote and Hunter (1996) point out, local government may not be held in high esteem but people do value local services and value local government more highly than central government. The poor record of a handful of local councils should not form the main case for centralizing public services and putting them into the hands of the 'new magistracy' which is neither elected nor, in some cases, has roots in the communities for which its members are responsible. In any case, local government has begun to transform itself and is experimenting with ways of enabling people to participate more fully as citizens rather than as periodic voters. Local democracy is being revitalized by changing the way local authorities operate and conduct their business. As part of this quiet revolution, local authorities are decentralizing decision-making, localizing services and increasing participation through neighbourhood forums. Decentralized local government therefore offers a participative and democratic framework for health authorities' functions. Rather than adopt the idea wholesale, a pilot scheme would seem the best way to proceed to test the feasibility of local government taking over the functions of health authorities.

A system of explicit national guidelines on priorities for treatment or a core set of guaranteed procedures would represent a pull to the centre thereby undermining the local purchaser role as patient's advocate, inhibiting clinical freedom, reducing patient choice and ending the notion of comprehensive health care. Rather than increasing the already excessive amount of centralization which is a feature of government in Britain, the aim ought to be to look for ways of devolving responsibility and allowing greater democratic influence over the whole process.

Muddling through elegantly does not mean a conservative defence of the *status quo* – this would be a good example of masterly inactivity. What muddling through elegantly acknowledges is that improvements are necessary in how decisions about priorities are made, especially at a micro level, but that these can be made within current arrangements. There is no need for a wholesale move to a nationally determined and led system of explicit rationing that is itself unproven and could prove damaging. Nobody denies that rationing gives rise to complex moral problems. But to face them explicitly in the manner that has been proposed by the rational rationers may just be too difficult for society to contemplate. Gillon (1994: xxvii) is surely right when he says:

Until there is far greater social agreement and indeed understanding of these exceedingly complex issues, I believe that it is morally safer to seek gradual improvement in our current methods of trying to reconcile the competing moral concerns – to seek ways of 'muddling through elegantly' as Hunter advocates, rather than to be seduced by systems that seek to convert these essentially moral choices into apparently scientific numerical methods and formulae.

If these 'technologies of distrust', are allowed to continue gnawing away at the traditional foundations of trust and support for public services like the NHS then the loser in the end will be the public (Miller 1996). Rational rationers are, regrettably and however well meaning, doing no one any favours if they contribute to such an outcome.

A concluding comment

When a new Labour government is grappling with a series of health-policy problems and challenges, it is timely to offer some advice on the subject of rationing based on the foregoing analysis. There will be a temptation for the government to wish to be seen to be acting rationally and decisively and to put its own distinctive stamp on a whole range of public policy matters. This is understandable, even laudable, but there is also a need to acknowledge – admittedly a rare characteristic among politicians – that not all problems are amenable to resolution especially through a technocratic approach. Health-care rationing is one of these problems. The available evidence demonstrates the limits to rationality in respect of the actions governments can reasonably be expected to take. I do not subscribe to the view but it is better to try even if unsuccessfully. There is a real danger that the 'cure' will kill the 'patient'.

The thrust and purpose of this discourse on the subject of rationing health care has been to alert all those involved in managing and providing health services, and perhaps also to those receiving them, to the need to exercise great caution when contemplating the use of techniques aimed at making rationing more explicit and subject to tight rules and procedures, possibly subject to public influence and scrutiny. The methodologies on display in Oregon and elsewhere, and evident also in QALYs and similar cost-utility techniques, are no more than intellectual constructs that incorporate particular values. They are not offering a neutral, technical or scientific means of making policy or determining priorities.

So much may be obvious but it bears constant restating because the seductive appeal of such techniques is considerable. Too often the means become ends in themselves and the value basis of seemingly hard numbers or formulae can quickly be forgotten by policy-makers anxious to find simple solutions to complex problems. As Gillon (1994: xxvii) puts it, health economists' techniques 'are tempting in their definitiveness and relative simplicity – but they fail to give value to the wide range of other potentially relevant moral concerns'. Consequently these other concerns are at risk of being overlooked.

It is a puzzling feature of the human condition that we subscribe to rationality and deplore, and wish above all to end, irrationality. We talk critically of implicit rationing and applaud explicit, open debate in the somewhat naïve hope, or belief, that out of this process better-informed decisions will emerge. But why should they? There is no real evidence, assuming it was possible even to agree on what would constitute reliable evidence, to substantiate the claim. One person's rationality is another's irrationality. Consequently, is it not the case that explicit rationing procedures are as vulnerable to subversion as implicit rationing mechanisms are to furthering the interests of certain individuals? We simply replace one set of interests – professionals – with another – vocal, middle-class élites – while marginal groups risk being further marginalized and excluded from the process.

The introduction of often half-understood technical devices on the part of policy-makers and those not expert in such matters will only serve to mystify and obfuscate discussions about priorities and, paradoxically, remove them further from public debate and democratic control. In short, the very means chosen to strengthen accountability and to empower the public could have quite the opposite result.

If this book carries a central message it is this: we should resist abandoning an admittedly imperfect though workable irrationality in favour of a spurious and possibly risky rationality for the reasons set out in this and preceding chapters. The need is to *satisfice*, in preference to seeking to *optimize*. As Mechanic (1995: 1659) argues, 'interest in making rationing explicit arises from the illusion that optimisation is possible'. Because there is no realistic alternative to satisficing, whether from a practical, political or moral standpoint, muddling through elegantly holds appeal, grounded as it is in pragmatic sensibility backed by a set of procedural rights governing the way individuals are treated and informed about decisions affecting them.

Muddling through elegantly offers no panaceas but, unlike the prescriptions offered by the rational rationers, nor does it seek to pretend to. Rather, it accepts that rationing is *a priori*, an unavoidably messy affair and always will be. But it nevertheless requires all those engaged in delivering and receiving health care to strive for a better way of deciding priorities, though without adopting the mantle of scientific rationality which is probably beyond society's grasp.

References

Aaron, H.J. and Schwartz, W.B. (1984) *The Painful Prescription: rationing hospital care*, The Bookings Institution, Washington DC.

Appleby, J., Walshe, K. and Ham, C. (1995) *Acting on the Evidence: a review of clinical effectiveness: sources of information, dissemination and implementation*. Research Paper Number 17, National Association of Health Authorities and Trusts, Birmingham.

Association of Metropolitan Authorities (1993) *Local Authorities and Health Services: the future role of local authorities in the provision of health services*, AMA, London.

Baker, R. (1995) 'Rationing, Rhetoric, and Rationality: a review of the health care rationing debate in America and Europe', in Humber, J.M. and Almeder, R.F., *Allocating Health Care Resources*. Biomedical Ethics Reviews 1994. Humana Press: New Jersey.

Barnard, K. (1991) 'Trends in Health Care: beyond market economics. A reflection on 40 years past and 10 years future', in Bengoa, R. and Hunter, D.J. (eds) *New Directions in Managing Health Care*. World Health Organization and The Nuffield Institute for Health Services Studies, Leeds.

Best, G. (1997) 'The Rationing Debate: confusion or conspiracy?', *Health Director*, 35, p. 13.

Bowling, A. (1996) 'Health Care Rationing: the public's debate', *British Medical Journal*, 312, pp. 670–4.

Bowling, A., Jacobson, B. and Southgate, L. (1993) 'Health Service Priorities: explorations in consultation of the public and health professionals on priority setting in an inner London health district', *Social Science and Medicine*, 37(7), pp. 851–7.

Boyd, K.M. (ed.) (1979) *The Ethics of Resource Allocation in Health Care*. Edinburgh University Press, Edinburgh.

British Medical Association (1995a) *Rationing Revisited: a discussion paper*, Health Policy and Economic Research Unit Discussion Paper No. 4, BMA, London.

British Medical Association (1995b) *Core Values for the Medical Profession in the 21st Century*, Report of a Conference, 3–4 November 1994, BMA, London.

Burns, H. (1996) *Making Outcomes Matter. Speaking Up No. 5*. National Association of Health Authorities and Trusts, Birmingham.

Bynoe, I. (1996) *Beyond the Citizen's Charter*, Institute for Public Policy Research, London.

Calabresi, G. and Bobbitt, P. (1978) *Tragic Choices*, Norton and Co., New York.

Califano, J.A. (1992) 'Rationing Health Care – the unnecessary solution', *University of Pennsylvania Law Review*, 140(5), pp. 1525–38.

Callahan, D. (1987) *Setting Limits: Medical Goals in an Aging Society*, Simon & Schuster, New York.

Calltorp, J. (1995) 'Sweden: no easy choices', in Maxwell, R.J. (ed.) *Rationing Health Care, British Medical Bulletin*, 51(4), pp. 791–8.

Carr-Hill, R.A. (1989) 'Assumptions of the QALY Procedure', *Social Science and Medicine*, 28, pp. 469–77.

Carr-Hill, R.A. (1991) 'Allocating Resources to Health Care: is the QALY a technical solution to a potential problem?', *International Journal of Health Services*, 21(2), pp. 351–63.

Carr-Hill, R.A. (1995) 'Editorial: Welcome? To the brave new world of evidence based medicine', *Social Science and Medicine*, 41(11), pp. 1467–8.

Carr-Hill, R.A. and Sheldon, T. (1992) 'Rationality and the Use of Formulae in the Allocation of Resources to Health Care', *Journal of Public Health Medicine*, 14, pp. 117–26.

Charlton, B. (1997) 'The Regulation of Evaluation and Development in Clinical Practice: a critique of "rationalist" general management in the "reformed" NHS', in Miles, A. (ed.) *Evaluation and Development in Clinical Practice*, The Royal Society of Medicine, London.

Clarke, M., Hunter, D.J. and Wistow, G. (1995) *Local Government and the NHS: the new agenda*, Local Government Management Board, Luton.

Clarke, M., Hunter, D.J. and Wistow, G. (1997) 'For Debate: local government and the NHS: the new agenda', *Journal of Public Health Medicine*, 19(1), pp. 3–5.

Coast, J. (1997) 'Rationing within the NHS should be Explicit: the case against', *British Medical Journal*, 314, pp. 1118–22.

Commission on Social Justice (1994) *Social Justice: strategies for national renewal*, Vintage, London.

Cooper, L., Coote, A., Davies, A. and Jackson, C. (1995) *Voices Off: tackling the democratic deficit in health*, Institute for Public Policy Research, London.

Coote, A. (1993) 'Public Participation in Decisions about Health Care', *Critical Public Health*, 4(1), pp. 36–49.

Coote, A. (1996) *Citizens' Juries*, Briefing notes prepared for King's Fund Seminar, 24 April, Institute for Public Policy Research, London.

Coote, A. and Hunter, D.J. (1996) *New Agenda for Health*, Institute for Public Policy Research, London.

Core Services Committee (1992) *Core Health and Disability Support Services for 1993/94*, Wellington.

Core Services Committee (1994) *The Core Debater*, 1, April, Wellington.

Cox, D. (1995) 'Ethics of Rationing Health Care Services', *British Medical Journal*, 310, pp. 261–2.

Daniels, N. (1992) 'Justice and Health Care Rationing: lessons from Oregon', in Strosberg, M.S., Wiener, J.M., Baker, R. and Fein, I.A. (eds) *Rationing America's Medical Care: the Oregon Plan and beyond*, The Brookings Institution, Washington DC.

Day, P. and Klein, R.E. (1983) 'The Mobilisation of Consent versus the Management of Conflict: decoding the Griffiths Report', *British Medical Journal*, 287, pp. 1813–15.

Dean, K. and Hunter, D.J. (1996) 'New Directions for Health: towards a knowledge base for public health action', *Social Science and Medicine*, 42(5), pp. 745–50.

Del Vecchio, M. (1997) 'Guaranteed Entitlement to Health Care', in Lenaghan, J. (ed.) *Hard Choices in Health Care: rights and rationing in Europe*, BMJ Publishing Group, London.

Department of Health (1994) *Code of Conduct and Code of Accountability for NHS Boards*, EL (94)40, Department of Health, London.

Department of Health and Social Security (1972) *Management Arrangements for the Reorganised NHS*, HMSO, London.

Department of Health and Social Security (1976) *Priorities for Health and Personal Social Services in England: a consultative document*, HMSO, London.

Department of Health and Social Security (1977) *Priorities in the Health and Social Services: the way forward*, HMSO, London.

Department of Health and Social Security (1981) *Care in Action: a handbook of policies and priorities for the health and personal social services in England*, HMSO, London.

Department of Health and Social Security and Welsh Office (1979) *Patients First: consultative paper on the structure and management of the NHS in England and Wales*, HMSO, London.

Dixon, J., Harrison, A. and New, B. (1997) 'Is the NHS Underfunded?' *British Medical Journal*, 314, pp. 58–61.

Dixon, J. and New, B. (1997) 'Editorial: setting priorities New Zealand-style', *British Medical Journal*, 314, pp. 86–7.

Dixon, J. and Welch, H.G. (1991) 'Priority Setting: lessons from Oregon', *The Lancet*, 337, pp. 891–4.

Doyal, L. (1995) 'How Not to Ration Health Care: the moral perils of utilitarian decision making', in Honigsbaum, F., Richards, J. and Lockett, T. *Priority Setting in Action: purchasing dilemmas*, Radcliffe Medical Press, Oxford.

Doyal, L. (1997) 'Rationing within the NHS should be Explicit: the case for', *British Medical Journal*, 314, pp. 1114–18.

Doyal, L. and Gough, I. (1991) *A Theory of Human Need*, Macmillan, Basingstoke.

Drummond, M., Torrance, G. and Mason, J. (1993) 'Cost-effectiveness League Tables: more harm than good', *Social Science and Medicine*, 37(1), pp. 33–40.

Eddy, D.M. (1994) 'Health System Reform: will controlling costs require rationing services?', *Journal of American Medical Association*, 272(4), pp. 324–8.

Finlayson, M. (1996) *An Analysis of the Implementation of Health Policy in New Zealand 1991–1996*, Unpublished DPhil Thesis, University of Waikato, Hamilton, New Zealand.

Flynn, R., Williams, G. and Pickard, S. (1996) *Markets and Networks: contracting in community health services*, Open University Press, Buckingham.

Fox, A. (1974) *Beyond Contract: work, power, and trust relations*, Faber & Faber, London.

Frankel, S.J. (1991) 'Health Needs, Health Care Requirements, and the Myth of Infinite Demand', *The Lancet*, 337, pp. 1588–9.

Frankford, D.M. (1994) 'Scientism and Economism in the Regulation of Health Care', *Journal of Health Politics, Policy and Law*, 19, pp. 773–99.

Freemantle, N. (1994) 'The Public and Professional Face of Rationing in the NHS', in Harrison, S. and Freemantle, N. (eds) *Working for Patients: Early Research Findings*, Nuffield Institute for Health, Leeds.

Freemantle, N. (1995) 'Dealing with Uncertainty: will science solve the problems of resource allocation in the UK NHS?', *Social Science and Medicine*, 40(10), pp. 1365–70.

Gafni, A. and Birch, S. (1991) 'Equality Considerations in Utility-based Measures of Health Outcomes in Economic Appraisals: an adjustment algorithm', *Journal of Health Economics*, 10, pp. 329–42.

Galbraith, J.K. (1993) *The Culture of Contentment*, Penguin Books, Harmondsworth.

Garland, M.J. (1992) 'Rationing in Public: Oregon's priority-setting methodology', in Strosberg, M.A., Wiener, J.M., Baker, R. and Fein, I.A. (eds) *Rationing America's Medical Care: The Oregon Plan and beyond*, The Brookings Institution, Washington DC.

Gerrard, K. and Mooney, G. (1993) 'QUALY League Tables: handle with care', *Health Economics*, 2, pp. 59–64.

Gillon, R. (ed.) (1994) *Principles of Health Care Ethics*, John Wiley and Sons, Chichester.

Gleisner, S. and Paterson, R. (1995) 'Rationing – the Role of Regional Health Authorities', *Health Manager*, 2(2), pp. 7–11.

Gormally, L. (1996) 'Rational Rationing or Reasonable Rationing?', unpublished text of a lecture.

Gray, A. and Jenkins, B. (1995) 'Public Management and the NHS', in Glynn, J.J. and Perkins, D.A. (eds) *Managing Health Care: challenges for the 90s.* W.B. Saunders, London.

Gray, S.F., Bevan, G. and Frankel, S. (1997) 'Purchasing Evidence: the corollary of evidence-based purchasing', *Journal of Public Health Medicine*, 19(1), pp. 6–10.

Griffiths, J. (1996) *Defining the Essential: the functions, roles and costs of health authorities and GP purchasers*, NHS Executive Anglia Oxford, North Thames and South Thames, London.

Griffiths, R. (1992) 'Seven Years of Progress: general management in the NHS', The Third Audit Commission Lecture 1991, *Health Economics*, 1(1), pp. 61–70.

Grimley Evans, J. (1993) 'Summary', in Grimley Evans, J., Goldacre, M.J., Hodkinson, H.M., Lamb, S. and Savory, M. *Health and Function in the Third Age. Papers Prepared for the Carnegie Inquiry into the Third Age*, Nuffield Provincial Hospitals Trust, London.

GRiPP (1994) *Getting Research into Practice and Purchasing: resource pack*, Anglia and Oxford Regional Health Authority, Oxford.

Grogan, C.M., Feldman, R.D., Nyman, J.A. and Shapiro, J. (1994) 'How Will We Use Clinical Guidelines? The experience of Medicare carriers', *Journal of Health Politics, Policy and Law*, 19, pp. 7–26.

Hadorn, D.C. and Holmes, A.C. (1997) 'The New Zealand Priority Criteria Project. Part 1: Overview', *British Medical Journal*, 314, pp. 131–4.

Ham, C. (1996) *Public, Private or Community: what next for the NHS?*, Demos, London.

Ham, C., Honigsbaum, F. and Thompson, D. (1993) *Priority Setting for Health Gain*, Department of Health, London.

Ham, C.J. (1981) *Policy Making in the NHS*, Macmillan, London.

Handy, C. (1994) *The Empty Raincoat*, Hutchinson, London.

Harrison, A., Dixon, J., New, B. and Judge, K. (1997) 'Funding the NHS: can the NHS cope in future?', *British Medical Journal*, 314, pp. 139–42.

Harrison, S., Hunter, D.J., Johnston, I., Nicholson, N., Thunhurst, C. and Wistow, G. (1991) *Health Before Health Care. Social Policy Paper Number 4*, Institute for Public Policy Research, London.

Harrison, S. (1988) *Managing the NHS: shifting the frontier?*, Chapman & Hall, London.

Harrison, S. (1997) 'Central Government should have a Greater Role in Rationing Decisions: the case against', *British Medical Journal*, 314, pp. 970–3.

Harrison, S. and Hunter, D.J. (1994) *Rationing Health Care*, Institute for Public Policy Research, London.

Harrison, S. and Lachmann, P. (1996) *Towards a High-Trust NHS*, Institute for Public Policy Research, London.

Harrison, S. and Pollitt, C. (1994) *Controlling Health Professionals: the future of work and organisation in the NHS*, Open University Press, Buckingham.

Harrison, S. and Wistow, G. (1997) *A Tale of Two Reports: the contribution to health and social care policy-making of Sir Roy Griffiths 1982–1992*. A Contribution to the ESRC Workshop on Comparative Biography and Administrative Leadership, unpublished paper, Leeds.

Harrison, S., Hunter, D.J., Marnoch, G. and Pollitt, C. (1992) *Just Managing: power and culture in the NHS*, Macmillan, Basingstoke.

Haywood, S.C. and Alaszewski, A. (1980) *Crisis in the Health Service: the politics of management*, Croom Helm, London.

Healthcare 2000 (1995) *UK Health and Healthcare Services: challenges and policy options*, Healthcare 2000, London.

Heclo, H. (1975) 'Social Politics and Policy Impacts', in Holden, Jr M. and Dresang, D.L. (eds) *What Government Does*, Sage, Beverly Hills.

Heclo, H. and Wildavsky, A. (1981) *The Private Government of Public Money*, Macmillan, Basingstoke.

Heginbotham, C. (1993) 'Health Care Priority Setting: a survey of doctors, managers, and the general public', in Smith, R. (ed.) *Rationing in Action*, British Medical Journal Publishing Group, London.

Hoggett, P. (1996) 'New Modes of Control in the Public Service', *Public Administration*, 74(1), pp. 9–32.

Honigsbaum, F. (1992) *Who Shall Live? Who Shall Die? Oregon's health financing proposals, King's Fund College Papers Number 4*, King's Fund College, London.

Honigsbaum, F., Richards, J. and Lockett, T. (1995a) *Priority Setting in Action: purchasing dilemmas*, Radcliffe Medical Press, Oxford.

Honigsbaum, F., Calltorp, J., Ham, C. and Holmstrom, S. (1995b) *Priority Setting Processes for Healthcare*, Radcliffe Medical Press, Oxford.

Hood, C. (1991) 'A Public Management for All Seasons?', *Public Administration*, 69(1), pp. 3–19.

House of Commons Health Committee (1995a) *Priority Setting in the NHS: purchasing, First Report, Session 1994–95, Volume 1 Report HC 134–1*, HMSO, London.

House of Commons Health Committee (1995b) *Priority Setting in the NHS: Purchasing, First Report, Session 1994–95, Volume II, Minutes of Evidence and Appendices, HC 134–II*, HMSO, London.

House of Commons Public Accounts Committee (1981) *Financial Control and Accountability in the NHS, Seventeenth Report, Session 1980–81, HC 255*, HMSO, London.

House of Commons Social Services Committee (1980) *The Government's White Papers on Public Expenditure: The Social Services. Third Report, Session 1979–80, Volume I HC 702*, HMSO, London.

House of Lords Select Committee on Science and Technology (1988) *Priorities in Medical Research*, Vol. 1, HMSO, London.

Howell, J.B.L. (1992) 'Re-examining the Fundamental Principles of the NHS', in *British Medical Journal, The Future of Health*, BMJ, London.

Hughes, D. and Griffiths, L. (1996) ' "But if you Look at the Coronary Anatomy . . .": risk and rationing in cardiac surgery', *Sociology of Health and Illness*, 18(2), pp. 172–97.

Hunt, P. (1993) 'Still Open to Question', *Health Service Journal*, 304, p. 21.

Hunter, D.J. (1980) *Coping with Uncertainty: policy and politics in the NHS*, Research Studies Press/John Wiley and Sons, Chichester.

Hunter, D.J. (1983) 'Centre-Periphery Relations in the NHS: facilitators or inhibitors of innovation?', in Young, K. (ed.) *National Interests and Local Government*, Joint Studies in Public Policy 7, Heinemann, London.

Hunter, D.J. (1984) 'Consensus Management or Chief Executives? Lessons from the NHS', *Local Government Studies*, May/June, pp. 39–50.

Hunter, D.J. (1992) 'Doctors as Managers: gamekeepers turned poachers?', *Social Science and Medicine*, 35(4), pp. 557–66.

Hunter, D.J. (1993a) *Rationing Dilemmas in Health Care, Research Paper Number 8*, National Association of Health Authorities and Trusts, Birmingham.

Hunter, D.J. (1993b) 'The Internal Market: the shifting agenda', in Tilley, I. (ed.) *Managing the Internal Market*, Paul Chapman Publishing, London.

Hunter, D.J. (1995a) 'Rationing Health Care: the political perspective', in Maxwell, R.J. (ed.) *Rationing Health Care, British Medical Bulletin*, 51(4), pp. 876–84.

Hunter, D.J. (1995b) 'Effective Practice', *Journal of Evaluation in Clinical Practice*, 1(2), pp. 131–4.

Hunter, D.J. (1996a) 'Rationing and evidence-based medicine', *Journal of Evaluation in Clinical Practice*, 2(1), pp. 5–8.

Hunter, D.J. (1996b) 'Evidence-based Medicine and Rational Rationing, *Journal of Clinical Effectiveness*, 1(4), pp. 134–6.

James, O. and Manning, N. (1996) 'Public Management Reform: a global perspective', *Politics*, 16(3), pp. 143–9.

Jenkins, S. (1995) *Accountable to None: the Tory nationalisation of Britain*, Hamish Hamilton, London.

Joint Working Party (1967) *The Shape of Hospital Management in 1980?* (Chairman: GPE Howard), King Edward's Hospital Fund for London, London.

Kennedy, I. (1993) 'Medicine in Society, Now and in the Future', in Lock, S. (ed.) *Eighty-five Not Out: essays in honour of Sir George Godber*, King's Fund, London.

Kitzhaber, J. and Kenny, A.M. (1995) 'On the Oregon Trail', in Maxwell, R.J. (ed.) *Rationing Health Care, British Medical Bulletin*, 51(4), pp. 808–18.

Klein, R. (1992a) 'Dilemmas and Decisions', *Health Management Quarterly*, xiv, pp. 2–5.

Klein, R.E. (1992b) 'Warning Signals from Oregon', *British Medical Journal*, 304, pp. 1457–8.

Klein, R. (1995) *The New Politics of the NHS*, 3rd edn, Longman, Harlow.

Klein, R. (1996) 'Commentary: The NHS and the New Scientism: solution or delusion?', *Quarterly Journal of Medicine*, 89, pp. 85–7.

Klein, R. (1997) 'Defining a Package of Healthcare Services the NHS is Responsible for: the case against', *British Medical Journal*, 314, pp. 506–9.

Klein, R. and Redmayne, S. (1992) *Patterns of Priorities: a study of the purchasing and rationing policies of health authorities, Research Paper Number 7*, National Association of Health Authorities and Trusts, Birmingham.

Klein, R., Day, P. and Redmayne, S. (1996) *Managing Scarcity: priority setting and rationing in the NHS*, Open University Press, Buckingham.

Larkin, G.V. (1993) 'Continuity in Change: medical dominance in the UK', in Hafferty, F.W. and McKinlay, J.B. (eds) *The Changing Medical Profession: an international perspective*, Oxford University Press, New York.

Lenaghan, J. (1996) *Rationing and Rights in Health Care*, Institute for Public Policy Research, London.

Lenaghan, J. (1997a) 'Central Government should have a Greater Role in Rationing Decisions: the case for', *British Medical Journal*, 314, pp. 967–70.

Lenaghan, J. (ed.) (1997b) *Hard Choices in Health Care: rights and rationing in Europe*, BMJ Publishing Group, London.

Lenaghan, J. (1997c) 'Citizens' Juries: towards best practice', *British Journal of Health Care Management*, 3(1), pp. 20–2.

Lenaghan, J. (1997d) 'Health Care Rights in Europe: a comparative discussion', in *Hard Choices in Health Care: rights and rationing in Europe*, BMJ Publishing Group, London.

Levinsky, N.G. (1990) 'Age as a Criterion for Rationing Health Care', *The New England Journal of Medicine*, 322, pp. 1813–16.

Light, D.W. (1997) 'The Real Ethics of Rationing' *British Medical Journal*, 315, pp. 112–15.

Long, A.F. and Eskin, F. (1995) 'The New Public Health: changing attitudes and practice', *Medical Principles and Practice*, 4, pp. 171–8.

Loughlin, M. (1996) 'Rationing, Barbarity and the Economist's Perspective', *Health Care Analysis*, 4, pp. 146–56.

Malcolm, L.A. (1997) Personal communication.

Malcolm, L.A. and Barnett, P. (1994) 'New Zealand's Health Providers in an Emerging Market', *Health Policy*, 29, pp. 85–100.

Marks, D.F. (1995) *NHS Reforms: the first three years: a survey of directors of public health*, Health Research Centre, Middlesex University, Middlesex.

Maxwell, R.J. (ed.) (1995) 'Rationing Health Care', *British Medical Bulletin*, 51(4), pp. 761–962.

May, A. (1993) 'Thatcherism, the New Public Management, and the NHS', in Light, D. and May, A. (eds) *Britain's Health System: from welfare state to managed markets*, Faulkner & Gray, Washington DC.

Maynard, A. (1996) 'Editorial: rationing health care', *British Medical Journal*, 313, p. 1499.

McKee, M. and Clarke, A. (1995) 'Guidelines, Enthusiasms, Uncertainty, and the Limits to Purchasing', *British Medical Journal*, 310, pp. 101–4.

McKee, M. and Figueras, J. (1996) 'Setting Priorities: can Britain learn from Sweden?', *British Medical Journal*, 312, pp. 691–4.

Mechanic, D. (1984) 'The Transformation of Health Providers', *Health Affairs*, 3, pp. 65–72.

Mechanic, D. (1986) *From Advocacy to Allocation: the evolving American health care system*, Free Press, New York.

Mechanic, D. (1995) 'Dilemmas in Rationing Health Care Services: the case for implicit rationing', *British Medical Journal*, 310, pp. 1655–9.

Miller, P. (1996) 'Dilemmas of Accountability: the limits of accounting', in Hirst, P. and Khilnani, S. (eds) *Reinventing Democracy*, Blackwell, Oxford.

Ministry of Health (1956) *The Cost of the National Health Service* (Guillebaud) Cmd 9663, HMSO, London.

Ministry of Welfare, Health and Cultural Affairs (1992) *Choices in Health Care. A Report by the Government Committee on Choices in Health Care, The Netherlands*, Ministry of Welfare, Health and Cultural Affairs, Rijswijk.

Mooney, G., Gerard, K., Donaldson, C. and Farrar, S. (1992) *Priority Setting in Purchasing: some practical guidelines, Research Paper Number 6,* National Association of Health Authorities and Trusts, Birmingham.

Moore, W. (1996) *Hard Choices: priority-setting in the NHS,* National Association for Health Authorities and Trusts, Birmingham.

Morone, J.A. (1993) 'The Health Care Bureaucracy: small changes, big consequences', *Journal of Health Politics, Policy and Law,* 18, pp. 723–39.

Mullen, P. (1995) *Is Health Care Rationing Really Necessary? Discussion Paper 36,* Health Services Management Centre, Birmingham.

National Association of Health Authorities and Trusts (1993) *Securing Effective Public Accountability in the NHS: a discussion paper,* NAHAT, Birmingham.

National Economic Research Associates (1994) *Financing Healthcare,* NERA, London.

New, B. (1996) 'The Rationing Agenda in the NHS', *British Medical Journal,* 312, pp. 1593–601.

New, B. and Le Grand, J. (1996) *Rationing in the NHS: principles and pragmatism,* King's Fund, London.

Newdick, C. (1995) *Who Should We Treat? Law, patients and resources in the NHS,* Oxford University Press, Oxford.

NHS Executive (1995) *Code of Practice on Openness in the NHS,* EL (95)60, NHS Executive, Leeds.

NHS Executive (1996) *Promoting Clinical Effectiveness: a framework for action in and through the NHS,* NHS Executive, Leeds.

NHS Management Executive (1992) *Local Voices: involving the local community in purchasing decisions,* NHS Management Executive, Leeds.

NHS Management Inquiry (1983) *Report* (Chairman: R. Griffiths), Department of Health and Social Security, London.

Peckham, M. (1991) 'Research and Development for the NHS', *The Lancet,* 338, pp. 367–71.

Percy-Smith, J. and Sanderson, I. (1992) *Understanding Local Needs,* Institute for Public Policy Research, London.

Pollitt, C.J. (1993) *Managerialism and the Public Services: cuts or cultural change?,* 2nd edn, Blackwell, Oxford.

Pollock, A.M., Brannigan, M. and Liss, Per-Erik (1995) 'Rationing Health Care: from needs to markets?', *Health Care Analysis,* 3, pp. 299–314.

Powell, J.E. (1966) *Medicine and Politics,* Pitman Medical, London.

Redmayne, S. (1995) *Reshaping the NHS: strategies, priorities and resource allocation, Research Paper Number 16,* National Association of Health Authorities and Trusts, Birmingham.

Redmayne, S. (1996) *Small Steps, Big Goals,* National Association of Health Authorities and Trusts, Birmingham.

Redmayne, S., Klein, R. and Day, P. (1993) *Sharing Out Resources: purchasing and priority setting in the NHS, Research Paper Number 11,* National Association of Health Authorities and Trusts, Birmingham.

Richardson, A. (1996) *Somerset Health – consulting the public,* Notes on Presentation to King's Fund Seminar, London.

Roberts, C., Crosby, D., Dunn, R., Evans, K., Grundy, P., Hopkins, R., Jones, J.H., Lewis, P., Vetter, N. and Walker, P. (1995) 'Rationing is a Desperate Measure', *Health Service Journal,* 105, p. 15.

Robinson, R. (1995) 'Health Economics and Priority Setting: nonsense on stilts?', in Honigsbaum, F., Richards, J. and Lockett, T. *Priority Setting in Action: purchasing dilemmas,* Radcliffe Medical Press, Oxford.

Robinson, R. and Le Grand, J. (eds) (1994) *Evaluating the NHS Reforms*, King's Fund Institute, London.

Rose, R. (1993) *Lesson-Drawing in Public Policy: a guide to learning across time and space*, Chatham House Publishers, New Jersey.

Rothman, D.J. (1992) 'Rationing Life', *The New York Review*, 5 March, pp. 32–7.

Royal College of Physicians (1995) *Setting Priorities in the NHS: a framework for decision-making*, Royal College of Physicians, London.

Royal Commission on the NHS (1979) *Report*, Cmnd 7615, HMSO, London.

Sackett, D.L. and Rosenberg, W.M.C. (1995) 'On the Need for Evidence-Based Medicine', *Health Economics*, 4, pp. 249–54.

Salmond, G. (1997) 'Health Sector Reform in New Zealand', *British Journal of Health Care Management*, 3(2), pp. 88–90.

Sartori, G. (1987) *The Theory of Democracy Revisited: Part One: The contemporary debate*, Chatham House Publishers, New Jersey.

Schut, F.T. (1996) 'Health Care Systems in Transition: The Netherlands. Part 1: Health Care Reform in The Netherlands: miracle or mirage?', *Journal of Public Health Medicine*, 18(3), pp. 278–84.

Scottish Health Services Council (1966) *Administrative Practice of Hospital Boards in Scotland* (Chairman: W.M. Farquharson-Lang), HMSO, Edinburgh.

Secretary of State for Health (1992) *The Health of the Nation: a strategy for health in England*, Cm 1986, HMSO, London.

Secretary of State for Health (1996) *The NHS: a service with ambitions*, Cm 3425, The Stationery Office, London.

Sheldon, T. and Long, A. (1994) *Report of Workshop on Clinical Effectiveness*, NHS Centre for Reviews and Dissemination, York.

Simon, H.A. (1957) *Administrative Behaviour*, Free Press, New York.

Smith, I. (1992) 'Ethics and Health Care Rationing: new challenges for the new public sector manager, *Journal of Management in Medicine*, 6, pp. 54–61.

Smith, R. (1991) 'Rationing: the search for sunlight', *British Medical Journal*, 303, pp. 1561–2.

Smith, R. (1995) 'Editorial: rationing: the debate we have to have', *British Medical Journal*, 310, p. 686.

St John, P. (1997) 'Market Forces Attack Cooperation in Health', *New Zealand Doctor*, 5 April.

Stewart, J. (1992) *Accountability to the Public*, European Policy Forum, London.

Strong, P. and Robinson, J. (1990) *The NHS under New Management*, Open University Press, Milton Keynes.

Swedish Parliamentary Priorities Commission (1995) *Priorities in Health Care: ethics, economy, implementation, Final Report*, Department of Health, Stockholm.

Tanenbaum, S.J. (1994) 'Knowing and Acting in Medical Practice: the epistemological politics of outcomes research, *Journal of Health Politics, Policy and Law*, 19, pp. 27–44.

Tanenbaum, S.J. (1995) 'Getting There from Here: evidentiary quandaries of the US outcomes movement', *Journal of Evaluation in Clinical Practice*, 1(2), pp. 97–103.

Tartaglia, A.P. (1992) 'Is Talk of Rationing Premature?', in Strosberg, M.A., Wiener, J.M., Baker, R. and Fein, I.A. (eds) *Rationing America's Medical Care: The Oregon Plan and Beyond*, The Brookings Institution, Washington DC.

Thompson, F.J. (1981) *Health Policy and the Bureaucracy: politics and implementation*, The MIT Press, Massachusetts.

Thorne, J.I. (1992) 'The Oregon Plan Approach to Comprehensive and Rational Health Care', in Strosberg, M.A., Wiener, J.M., Baker, R. and Fein, I.A. (eds) *Rationing America's Medical Care: the Oregon plan and beyond*, The Brookings Institution, Washington DC.

Timmins, N. (1996) 'NHS "wastes £1bn on ineffective treatments"', *The Independent*, 2 January.

Tudor Hart, J. (1994) *Feasible Socialism: the NHS past, present and future*, Socialist Health Association, London.

Van de Ven, W.P.M.M. (1995) 'Choices in Health Care: a contribution from The Netherlands', in Maxwell, R.J. (ed.) *Rationing Health Care, British Medical Bulletin*, 51(4), pp. 781–90.

van der Grinten, T.E.D. (1996) 'Scope for Policy: essence, operation and reform of the policy of Dutch health care', in Gunning-Schepers, L. (ed.) *Fundamental Questions about the Future of Health Care*, Schu Hofgevers.

van der Grinten, T.E.D. (1997) personal communication.

van der Made, J. and Maarse, H. (1997) 'Access to Health Care in The Netherlands', in Lenaghan, J. (ed.) *Hard Choices in Health Care: rights and rationing in Europe*, BMJ Publishing Group, London.

Vickers, Sir G. (1965) *The Art of Judgement: a study of policy making*, Chapman & Hall, London.

Walker, P. (1997) 'The Poverty of Professionalism', *The Public Health Physician*, 8(1), pp. 2–4.

Walshe, K. and Ham, C. (1997) *Acting on the Evidence: progress in the NHS*, The NHS Confederation, Birmingham.

Wennberg, J.E. (1990) 'Outcomes Research, Cost Containment, and the Fear of Health Care Rationing', *The New England Journal of Medicine*, 323, pp. 1202–4.

Wildavsky, A. (1979) *The Art and Craft of Policy Analysis*, Macmillan, London.

Williams, A.H. (1985) *Medical Ethics: health service efficiency and clinical freedom*, Nuffield/York Portfolio Number 2, Nuffield Provincial Hospitals Trust, London.

Williams, A.H. (1997) 'Rationing Health Care by Age: the case for', *British Medical Journal*, 314, pp. 820–2.

World Health Organization (1996) *European Health Care Reforms: analysis of current strategies*, WHO Regional Office for Europe, Copenhagen.

Zimmern, R. (1996) *Beyond Effectiveness: the appropriateness of clinical care – what needs to happen now*, transcript of a speech to the National Medical Directors and Directors of Public Health Meeting, November.

INDEX

Printed and bound by CPI Group (UK) Ltd, Croydon, CR0 4YY

01/11/2024

01782615-0006